TWO OR THREE
GATHERED TOGETHER

OTHER BOOKS BY GLENN CLARK

TWO OR THREE
GATHERED TOGETHER

by

GLENN CLARK

Published by

HARPER & BROTHERS

New York and London

Contents

Contents

I. A Vision

For some time I have felt, through one of those interior admonitions that have never failed me, that there was a great yearning for God in the souls of men, ready to take form in some concerted action, a sort of ground swell of devotion, and that the time has come to unite all our spiritual forces behind it. Concurrent with that thought there has come to me a letter from Kagawa and his friends in Japan with the plea that some of us who believe profoundly in prayer become the spearhead for a Kingdom of God Movement in America and the world. Muriel Lester, on her trip across America to see Gandhi, had some long talks with me, and seconded this wish.

I breathed this vision into a little prayer, and the prayer gathered a response both from God and from man which has been tremendous. Around us I found such marvelous spiritual souls as Rufus Jones, Winifred Kirkland, Kirby Page, Sherwood Eddy, Bishop Anderson, Bishop Hobson, Zona Gale, Arthur Holt, E. Stanley Jones, Harry Emerson Fosdick, Roger Babson, John R. Bunting, William Boddy, Franz Aust,

Jim Hardwick, Glenn Harding, Dan Fleming, George Washington Carver, Dad Elliot, Jesse R. Wilson, and hundreds of others. Because of the representative character of the leaders, but above all because of the tremendous response of thousands of praying people scattered all over the nation and all over the world, God has made it clearly evident that He has given us the background and the foundation for building this Movement with quiet confidence that we shall not be building in vain. If we contact the springs of spiritual power in the hearts of praying men and women all over the world deeply enough, we shall witness God re-creating civilization and bringing nations to rebirth.

This Movement is to be an interior Movement, hardly deserving the title of Movement, but infinitely more significant than any outer movement could ever be. It is to be a mere seed, a mere wish, a mere soul's sincere desire, given completely into the Father's hands. It is to be a prayer in which two or three thousand, perhaps two or three million, will agree to give their nation and their world completely over to Almighty God with absolute trust in Him for the ultimate and correct solution of all their problems. At times the Movement, just like a seed, will be completely out of sight; sometimes, like a blade of wheat, it will appear above the ground; but whether visible or invisible, it will always be growing and perhaps never growing so powerfully as when completely buried out of sight of the eyes of men.

In the second place, it is to be a Movement without a name, as nearly as such a Movement can be said to exist without a name. The name which most of those associated with its beginning have ascribed to it is indeed a name above all names save that of God Himself, a name too sacred to be lightly bandied about in committee rooms, or placed on programs, or sent promiscuously through the mail on letterheads— a name at once too precious and too universal for any single group or sect to claim, or even appear to claim, as their own. But if we take special care that this Movement never becomes a sect in any sense of the word, but takes in all sects, that it never becomes a Movement which is dependent upon committee meetings, program announcements, and formal letterheads, but remains primarily an interior Movement for the nourishing of the souls of men, then and then only will it deserve the title that many claim for it—"The Kingdom of God Movement for the World." Long before the early followers of Christ were called Christians, they humbly called themselves "Children of the Way." This or some other appellation comes near the extreme simplicity many of our friends crave especially at the outset, and which we shall fall back upon whenever any misuse or misunderstanding occurs in the use of other titles that may be attached to us.

In the third place, it is to be a leaderless Movement, as far as any Movement, having unity of purpose and cohesion of action, can be said to be leaderless. The real leader will be Christ. All the rest of us will be servants, and those who are called into council or who are sent on journeys, must be the most surrendered servants of all. So deep must be the surrender of those who participate in the planning of the Movement that they will be willing to step aside for other participants whenever the best interests so indicate.

We are not *starting* this Movement. No one is starting it. We are merely stepping into the current of a great unfolding Movement that God has already started quietly and inconspicuously in the hearts of men. When God starts a Movement He first plants it in the heart of a man. It then spreads to another, then to three, then to six, and so on to twelve, twenty-four, forty-eight, and finally to thousands or millions. Many praying souls in America have been serving as such focal points for bringing the Kingdom of God into the hearts of men for a long time. Out of sight of the average man, something very powerful has been going on under the surface of things. Like all healthy, organic growth, which starts with one cell, then divides into two, and these subdivide into four, so these praying individuals have been dividing and subdividing; in other words, they have been "multiplying by losing themselves in God and others," until in the fullness of time there now comes into view the vision of all these scattered groups uniting for one great vision of God.

This, in essence, is the Kingdom of God Movement. Radiating influences from this Christ-filled life and that Christ-filled life meet and coalesce and spread again until all the world is being filled with Christ. All that is now necessary, as one spiritual leader writes, is for all these praying people to find each other out. So I am requesting that you join your prayers with the rest of us that Christ may enter into the hearts of us all, and that all men will be led captive to the spirit of the Love of God in all walks of life, from the inmost to the outermost, from the mystic inner experience of God to the outermost expression of that experience in which all men may be given opportunity for finding complete self-expression in worshiping and serving God and in loving and serving man.

Remember, this is not so much a Movement as an overflowing of the abundance of love and faith that fills our hearts. Without this abundance "within us" there would be no Movement possible "outside of us." Therefore, the one thing needful is the filling of our hearts with this overflowing of love and faith. This done, all is done. Unlimited good will ensue, if out of this overflowing there shall be brought about a uniting of all praying people of all creeds and of all faiths all over the broad world. There is unlimited power in united, earnest prayer.

Therefore, the first step, and the most indispensable step in the inauguration of this Movement is to hold it in our hearts as a Vision. For nothing worth doing was ever done which was not preceded by a Dream.

II. A Dream

Before we start upon this journey, let us dream together. And let us dream as little children would dream, for have we not been told by the greatest Dreamer of all time that unless we turn and become as children we shall in no wise be worthy to enter into the Kingdom of Heaven? "For verily I say unto you that the angels of little children are always looking upon the face of the Father." So pull down from the shelf the old book of fairy stories that thrilled your childhood, and open the pages to the story of Cinderella, the little girl whose dream came true.

And why did her dream come true? First of all, because she *had a right to dream*. She was the *real* daughter of her *real* Father, and although momentarily expropriated, she was actually sitting in her Father's house. The stepsisters, you may remember, did not have dreams that came true, because they were usurpers and counterfeits, and were not the authentic daughters of the Father of the house. No amount of "step-dreaming," "step-visioning," or "step-praying" can ever take the place of real dream-

[7]

ing and real praying, any more than powders and perfumes and costly raiment when placed on the outside of a person, can alter the lineage of his inner soul. So Cinderella's dream came true because she knew that her relationship to her Father was real.

In the second place, Cinderella *loved* her dream. She warmed her dream before the open fireplace. Probably more great ideas have been thought out in the cozy warmth of the open fire than anywhere else. The open fireplace is a symbol. A dream cannot have power until it is warmed in the flame of our own deep love and desire.

In the third place, she *relinquished* her dream. Having the clear picture of her heart's desire she let go of it and let it go up the chimney, only to reappear beside her in the room in a most unexpected form—the form of a fairy godmother.

So we learn that after one has recognized his sonship to the Father, after he has desired and loved his vision, he must vaporize it and relegate it to the unfathomed depths of the unseen, the place which in our childhood days we called Fairyland.

When the fairy godmother speaks she announces the fourth law of the dream that comes true. She tells Cinderella that she may go to the ball and dance with the charming prince, but this fulfillment is granted upon one condition and one condition only. She can stay at the dance only as long as the hands of the clock move upward toward the zenith, toward heaven and away from earth. By this fairy code she was revealing that as long as a dream can dance with an upward lilt, that is to say, with the spirit of unselfishness and love and joy and peace, one may continue to dream it and dance with it, but the moment one lets his vision turn downward toward doubt, despair, pride or greed, all its beautiful garments will turn to rags and tatters and he will find himself like a scullion at the banquet of a king. Does not Jesus tell about a wedding guest who was cast out from the feast into outer darkness because his garment betrayed that his soul was not in the wedding spirit? Cinderella obeyed all these rules and her dream came true. All went perfectly that night with one slight exception. She overstayed her time just one second. So engrossed was she in her dream that she allowed the midnight hour to strike, and one of her glass slippers remained caught upon the stair.

This brings us to the fifth and final law of the dream: that *the dream*, if it is properly dreamed, *will ultimately find its dreamer out.*

The story ended, as you may remember, with a long search by the prince for his charming and beautiful partner. Every woman in the kingdom was required to have the slipper tried on her foot. Even Cinderella, much to her sisters' disgust, was summoned from the kitchen hearth and commanded by the herald to meet the test. The sisters were so ambitious to be queen, that one was willing to have a toe cut off and the other a part of a heel. But that is not the way to make dreams come true. It is beginning at the wrong end. If it is *your* dream, it will fit *you*; otherwise all the doctors in the kingdom can carve the outside of you in vain. And so Cinderella was discovered at last, and she found the "Prince Charming" waiting for her, and the dream of her heart came into perfect fulfillment.

If you follow this method of dreaming even though you seem to fail, even though you leave your glass slipper behind you, you will find that you have not failed. Your apparent failures will ultimately help to bring you to success, provided you have dreamed your dream aright. If the dreamer holds fast to his dream, THE DREAM WILL ULTIMATELY FIND THE DREAMER OUT. Was that not true of Joseph, of Daniel and of Abraham Lincoln? Was it not true of all the great dreamers of all the world?

In a day when most people took for granted that our nation must always remain half slave and half free, Abraham Lincoln dreamed a dream of a nation entirely free, a nation of the people, by the people, and for the people. Douglas, who believed in compromise and equivocation, did not share this dream. Lincoln put his dream into words and gave expression to it in his famous debates with Douglas, and by so doing, he lost the senatorship of Illinois.

But when the Republican party began searching for a man who stood four-square for a free and united nation, they found in the very incident that led to Lincoln's failure to win the senatorship of Illinois, the glass slipper that was ultimately to win for him the presidency of the United States. They went from statesman to statesman to see who believed deep down in his heart that a "nation cannot live half slave and half free." Seward would gladly have cut off part of the "heel" of his prim conservatism if he would be allowed to wear the glass slipper. Douglas would gladly have cut off his enlarged "toe" of squatter sovereignty if that would help him wear the slipper. All to no avail. Finally Lincoln was found sitting among the ashes of his previous defeats, holding fast to his vision. The dream of a united people fitted his foot exactly, and he became the standard-bearer and later the greatest President and the greatest public man America has ever produced. The way to greatness, the way to achievement, the way to constructive creative action of any kind is through the door of a dream, properly dreamed and persistently held fast to.

"Give me Scotland or I die!" cried John Knox, and that voice, although it may have been no louder than a whisper, because it voiced a dream that had been properly dreamed, was heard all over Scotland. For when the day of reform finally came, Scotland passed by the bishops and the elders, who had proved but unworthy stepdaughters of the church, and found that the dream of a spiritually repentant nation fitted the foot of this indomitable preacher of Scotland.

"And what shall I say more? For the time would fail me to tell of Gideon and of Barak and of Samson, and of Jephthah, of David also, and Samuel and of the prophets."

Although it is a long step from the fairy tale of Cinderella to the tale of our great idealists like Knox and Lincoln, it is still a further step to the tale of our great practical and hardheaded realists like the builders of factories and the producers of airplanes and automobiles today. Our modern civilization has been created by water and gas which is first heated, then vaporized, and finally turns all the machinery of the world. But while these successive steps are adhered to as faithfully as the ancients followed the laws of the Medes and the Persians, our great industrial leaders don't seem to know the fourth rule of the code—that they must not let this material machinery dance after the midnight hour of selfishness and hate and greed has struck in their hearts. The proper understanding and application of this rule of the code is neglected because the homes and the schools and the churches have failed to inculcate in the hearts of men today the principles of that greatest dreamer of all time . . . Jesus of Nazareth. These physical inert elements of coal and iron and gas and water are subject to the same midnight peril of the Cinderella dream if dreamed unwisely, as our tragic dance with them in the midnight hour of 1914-18 so vividly reminds us! And are we not still dancing with those forces after the midnight hour of selfishness and greed of 1929-42?

III. Jesus' Dream

And now I shall sum up all that we have discovered
by letting you hear the story of Cinderella as Jesus
would tell it. For Jesus, that greatest Dreamer of us
all, was a teller of fairy stories . . . the kind of
fairy stories, however, that always come true. And
the greatest story He ever told was a Cinderella
story. In the Jesus story, however, the Cinderella was
a man, not a girl, and the Cinderella man brought
his misfortune upon himself, and did not have to
depend upon the machinations of an unkindly step-
mother to bring it upon him. And after he had,
through his own selfishness and folly, expropriated
himself from his father's house, he was found sitting amid the husks (instead of the cinders) and
looking into a campfire upon the heath beside a
pigpen (instead of a fire within the grate in his
father's house). His dream, like that of Cinderella's,
was of finding union with Love, although the ob-
ject of that Love with him was his father instead of
the Prince Charming.

But he followed perfectly the Cinderella code.

First, he remembered that he was a real son of his real father: "He came to himself." Second, he warmed his dream in his love and desire: "How many servants of my father have bread enough and to spare and I perish here from hunger! I will arise and go to my father." Third, he vaporized it and let it go: "I shall say unto my father, I am not worthy to be called thy son. Make me as one of thy hired servants." Fourth, the fairy godmother (or the inner hunch of guidance) came to him with unmistakable power, and he arose and went to his father.

And now the danger spot enters into the dream of the Prodigal Son, exactly where it entered into the dream of Cinderella. As he walks or dances along the road toward the fulfillment of his vision, he is tempted to let the midnight bell of selfishness and conceit and falsehood ring in his heart. He is tempted to change his story as he goes along and make it a story of pride and self-justification instead of one of penitence and humility. But he casts these temptations aside. He holds fast to the upward swing of his vision. Long before the midnight hour has struck he arrives at his father's house. Immediately upon his arrival the dream, as all dreams that move in accordance with this inner code, comes instantly and amazingly true. Above the penitent cry of the prodigal son, above the critical voice of the

elder brother, above the sound of music and dancing, rings the voice of the triumphant father: "Bring
forth the best robe and put it on him, and put a
ring on his hand, and shoes on his feet. And bring
hither the fatted calf and kill it; and let us eat and
be merry. For this my son was dead, and is alive,
again; he was lost and is found."

As with Cinderella they placed "shoes on his feet,"
only in this case it was not a glass slipper, but a
sandal. And the sandal fitted his foot. We can be
sure of that. And it probably fitted the foot of no
one else. During all the long years of the prodigal's
wandering, the Father had carefully kept his son's
sandals ready and waiting for his return. Had he remained away ten, twenty, or even thirty years they
would have been waiting still. Yes, our slippers and
sandals identify us, but no more than do our visions
and our dreams. Trust to your dream and it will
ultimately find you out. For the dream will always
wait until its own dreamer comes to claim it, no
matter how long he defers the coming.

What were the greatest dreams ever dreamed in
the history of man? Two there are that stand out
as eagles among birdlings. Let us consider these two.

Our Bible is divided into two Testaments, and
each Testament centers around a dream. The dream
of the Old Testament is of a Redeemer that is to

come some day and save Israel and the entire world from the suffering and sin in which it is submerged. The entire Old Testament is given over to that dream, from the cry of Job, "For I know that my Redeemer liveth, and that He shall stand at the latter day upon the earth and represent me before God," to the glowing words of Isaiah, "And his name shall be called Wonderful, Counselor, The Mighty God, The Everlasting Father, The Prince of Peace." In every age the prophet shaded his eyes and scanned the horizon to discern the coming of the anointed One. Every mother in Judea had a dignity not shared by women of other nations, because she might become, by the grace of God, the mother of this marvelous son of God.

And out of that dream, dreamed by an entire nation for thousands of years, there at last emerged the fulfillment of the dream . . . Jesus of Nazareth. Jesus was the greatest Dream ever dreamed by mankind. And had a nation not dreamed the Dream for hundreds of years before He came, Jesus Himself might never have come.

When I say Jesus was a Dream, I don't want to give the impression that He didn't exist. Our dreams are always our greatest realities. When I say Jesus was the world's greatest Dream, I do not imply that He was an illusion. A nation lives by its dreams;

it dies by its illusions. A dream is the most solid, the most real, the most permanent thing that exists; an illusion is the most unreal, and the most impermanent. George Washington was the dream of the American colonies come true; Benedict Arnold was its illusion. Alfred the Great was the dream of England; George III was the illusion. Tolstoy dreamed a dream with his peasants; was Lenin the fulfillment of that dream or was he an illusion? Napoleon, as long as he was a devoted servant of the ideals of the republic of France, was a dream come true; but when he began to glorify only Napoleon he became an illusion. That explains why Jesus of Nazareth is the greatest Dream of the ages. He will never fade from the place He holds in the hearts of men, for He said, "I seek not mine own will, but the will of the Father which hath sent me."

Then after Jesus came, He too dreamed a dream. He dreamed a dream that filled the entire New Testament, even as the dream of His coming had filled the Old Testament. Let us pause before this thought. Jesus, the greatest incarnation of a dream of all the ages, Himself dreamed another dream! A dream within a dream! Can anything be more powerful, more invisible, more deeply embedded in the central heart of life itself? And what was the dream

that Jesus dreamed? JESUS DREAMED OF THE KING-
DOM OF GOD COMING INTO FULFILLMENT ON EARTH.

He began his Sermon on the Mount with the statement, "Blessed are the poor in spirit for of such is
the *Kingdom of Heaven*." The climax of the Sermon on the Mount was, "Seek ye first the *Kingdom
of God* and His righteousness and all these things
shall be added unto you." The center of the Lord's
Prayer contains the words, "Thy Kingdom come, on
earth as it is in heaven."

*Let us all unite together in dreaming this great
dream with Jesus.* Today, like Cinderella, we sit
among the ashes of the hates and rivalries of com-
peting and warring nations; like the Prodigal Son
we sit amidst the husks of an overmaterialized, over-
mechanized world. Is it not time that we came to
ourselves and arose and went to our Father? Before we start on this journey, let us be still awhile
and vision as clearly as possible just what such a
Movement back to the Father would imply.

IV. Our Dream Becomes Jesus' Dream

First of all, we shall vision this Movement as a
Jesus Movement. No one who loves, adores, wor-
ships or venerates Jesus is to be left out. Anyone
who loves Jesus of Nazareth belongs to us and we
belong to him. But this loving and adoring and
venerating is not to be given to a paper Jesus, a book
Jesus, a Jesus smothered in creeds and dogmas . . .
but to a living Jesus. The only creed that Jesus
laid down as an indispensable working faith was
God our Father, all men brothers, and Love the law
of Life. He embodied these principles so completely
in His own life that merely to look at Jesus, to
follow Him, to open our hearts to Him and to let
Him enter and possess us, will solve all the problems of our lives. As Jesus *lived* these principles,
let us do our best to *live Jesus*.

This means that the second characteristic of this
Movement is that it is to be a Love Movement. Jesus
said God is not a definition, God is Love. And Love
is not a word to be professed, but a word to be lived.
Therefore the central purpose of our Movement is

to spread among men the contagion of living the life of Love. Because the word Love has been used so loosely among many people, let us make clear the characteristics of the kind of Love that is to be at the heart and kernel of this Movement. This Love which reached its zenith in the life of Jesus is a divine Love, a Love that is willing to lay down its life for its friend. The chief characteristic of Jesus' Love was its spontaneity and its wholeness. "I came to make men whole," said Jesus, and He was able to do this because His Love was WHOLE. Even virtue can assume the likeness of evil when it is broken into fragments, becomes fanatic, morbid, or captive to some fragmentary conception of itself. This Wholeness of Love, on the other hand, is always healing, strengthening, contagious, irresistible, and wonderful. The three chief characteristics of this Wholeness of Love as Jesus expressed it, and as we should emulate Him, are the following:

First of all, it must be a very sincere Love. This Movement is to be a banding together of people who have actually found Love to be the greatest force in their lives, and out of their authentic experience of Love toward God and Man, are able and willing to gamble their lives upon the proposition that Love— understanding Love, audacious Love, sacrificial Love —if given a free hand in our individual lives and in affairs of state, can settle all the problems that this human race is heir to. Unless this Love is sincere, unless one has learned the power of it and the sweetness of it in his own life, all this talk about it is but a sounding brass and clanging cymbal and he becomes an impediment instead of a help in this Movement of Christ. Those who throw themselves into the Movement must do so with the audacity of that apostle who said, "Whether there be prophecies, they shall fail, whether there be tongues, they shall cease, whether there be knowledge, it shall vanish away, BUT LOVE NEVER FAILETH."

In the second place, our Love must be a very humble Love. It must vaunt not itself, be not puffed up. This Movement, if it be truly a Christ Movement, must joyously serve all other movements that are constructively spiritual and Christlike, helping every church, every sect, every creed. We who are associated with it claim no exclusive, private pipe line to God. We do not claim that our formulation, nor do we claim that the way we live our faith, is without flaws or as perfect as the way others may live their faith.

In the third place, this Love must be a very tolerant Love. This Movement which is dedicated completely to the Christ Way "is not easily provoked, thinketh no evil . . . endureth all things." The tendency to belittle other groups that don't happen to use the same ritual or technique as ours . . . that spirit of self-righteousness which Henry Drummond calls "the vice of the virtuous" . . . has created more skeptics, atheists, and bitter haters of the church than all the opponents of religion put together. "He who is not against us is for us," said Jesus, and that can well be the watchword of the Love that we have in our hearts. If a Love be a WHOLE LOVE it is among other things an understanding Love. As soon as any one group gets close enough to another group so that they can see the inner experiences out of which that movement grew, they can always see something good in it to love and some extenuating circumstances that enable them to forgive that which they cannot love.

The service of this Movement is not a service of proselyting but a service of contagion. In formulation and execution it may have much to forgive. But in so far as it is filled with the true Christ spirit it can share with all other movements in furthering the Kingdom of God. We are to make Christ contagious first. After that we can leave the settling of controversies concerning details to the slower working out of human experience. A careful study of history will prove, I believe, that most great movements were retarded, rather than aided, by the use of force, whether on the battlefield or in the pulpit.

Finally, THIS IS A KINGDOM OF GOD MOVEMENT. The message that Jesus preached from morning to night, from seedtime to harvest, from the beginning of His active ministry to the very end was concerning a vast, perfect conception of living the beautiful life now and here, which He called the Kingdom of God.

This conception of the beautiful life as Jesus presented it has two facets: first, the personal, mystic, inner experience of God, and Oneness with the Christ consciousness; and, second, the reforming, re-adjusting, and revitalizing of the processes of society so that the spirit of brotherhood and love may have unhindered opportunity for perfect expression. Perhaps no one blends these two phases in his own life and teaching in our modern times any better than the one whose suggestion started this Movement into being—Toyohiko Kagawa.

Because one of the central principles of this Movement is that all growth comes from within, and therefore the whole process of action is from the secret inner vision into the visible outward mani-festation, this Movement concerns itself first and foremost with the inner spiritual experiencing of God and practicing His presence in our personal

and individual lives. Attain that perfectly and uni-
versally enough, and the outer manifestation of the
improved social order will take care of itself.

The guidance that comes to those who are in this
Movement is that whatever that outer social action
shall be that we undertake, we are to act upon the
highest light we have, and to act gently, lovingly,
putting Love above everything else, even above
courage and zeal, knowing that only as Love grows
perfectly clear, unconfined, released and pure, can
courage and zeal detach themselves sufficiently from
that which they are so often associated with . . .
fanaticism and intolerance . . . and become converted into the true valor of the Soul.

V. The Replanting of the Dream

It was seven years ago that I wrote the preceding chapters which you have just finished reading. I have a purpose now in reproducing them, exactly as I wrote them then. For it has been my experience that a dream has to be planted as a seed, the harvest must be reaped, and the new seed planted, and not until several replantings is the complete realization of the dream made possible. A man dreams of a forest and plants an acorn. Many years later the tree is sufficiently grown to bear acorns of itself. He gathers all the acorns that fall from this tree and plants them on many acres of land. Out of this second planting, and not until then, does his dream of a forest come true.

In the seven years that have elapsed the oak tree has grown, and a new crop of acorns is on hand. *The time to plant the forest has come.*

As I wrote the preceding chapters, it did not seem that I had written them, but as though a Hand reaching over my shoulder was writing them through me. It was as though I, myself, were the pen in some Other and Greater Hand, and that all I have here recorded on these preceding pages was recorded by Someone Else, for some larger purpose than I myself could conceive. Everything about this Movement was to be so detached, so transparent, so unframed and so unorganized that at first glance one would be inclined to wonder how it could move ahead, accomplish anything, even get under way. There were three definite things that did come out of it, however, which did give opportunity for some concrete, practical action.

Very clear leading came that this Movement was to give itself to three definite, distinct forms of expression: first, *the Quiet Hour* for cultivating the vital experience of God in each individual heart; second, *the Prayer Group* for cultivating the expression of vital, co-operative prayer with others; third, the opening of avenues for bringing the strength and inspiration of the Quiet Hour and of the Prayer Group into vital, constructive expression in the *social movements of the day*.

I thought about these a long time, I prayed about them, I tried to find out from God whether there should be anything added or anything subtracted, but nothing "came through." As this was to be a Jesus Movement, a Love Movement, all that we could do about it, therefore, was to plant the idea as a seed. We might occasionally water it, and cultivate it, but we must leave all the growing, all the unfolding, all the fruit bearing, all the achieving of results, to the Father of Infinite Love. Those participating in the Movement were all to be Junior Partners, and their share was to look after the intention, and the intention only; the Senior Partner, and He alone, would be concerned and responsible for the results.

Before we start out upon this venture, it would be well for us to pause a moment and make an inventory of what will be demanded of us. "For which of you," said Jesus, "desiring to build a tower, doth not first sit down and count the cost, whether he have wherewith to complete it?" We must ourselves be so surrendered to Christ that we are utterly and entirely His before we can ever take thought together in regard to the steps we should take. The picture of the scrambled world cannot be put into order until we have straightened out the picture of the scrambled man on the opposite side.

My first concern was to see whether my own intentions were clear as crystal, so clear that nothing of self could cast a shadow over the slightest part of my work. I must become so clear, that, in the words of Evelyn Underhill, "the naked soul could follow the naked Christ." I must see the perfect soul in everyone, no matter how thick the shell of Ego might seem to be, I must trust myself to everyone and be worthy to let each one trust himself to me. I must start living in this Kingdom of Heaven right *here* and *now*. There must be no qualification, no subterfuge, no reservation whatsoever. I must give as much time to the meanest sinner as to the highest soul. But I must not, on the other hand, out of false humility, avoid the highest soul if there was some reason for us to come together and if he was willing to accept me.

As months went on I learned many things. I learned, for instance, that there were some degrees of sin where I could not help as much as others who had had some actual experience in that form of sin. I found that there were some forms of trouble foreign to my experience where I could not help as much as others could help. There were some places where my love would be mistaken for weakness, some places where my outgiving would feed the weakness of others and not their strength. All this taught me humility and wisdom, two of the most essential of graces, and it also taught me the need of co-operating with others, and sharing the burdens of the Kingdom message with others who were stronger than I.

On the other hand, there were some forms of sickness where my faith rose to the height of mountains and the trouble became as helpless as a moth before a flame of light. There were some forms of sin where I could take the sinner by the hand and lead him straight to the Cross of Christ and witness his sin roll completely away, as though it had never been.

And above all, I found that God had especially given me the gift and the training to be used as an instrument of His Love for breaking down barriers between all forms of religious thought and religious thinkers, and bring them into harmony and understanding. It became a passion of mine to make the whole army of Christ of one mind and one blood. For instance, while I was an elder in the Presbyterian Church, I taught a Bible Class in a Congregational church and spoke from pulpits of Methodist, Baptist, and Friend groups all over the land. While I had attended Catholic services only three or four times in my life a leading Catholic priest reviewed *The Soul's Sincere Desire* in a distinguished Catholic magazine, closing with the words, "While the author is one of our *estranged brethren*, there is nothing in this book that will hurt the devout Catholic; it breathes the spirit of Brother Lawrence and St. Francis of Assisi."

Although I have attended Christian Scientist Meetings only three times in my life, I found that Christian Scientists everywhere were reading my books; and before long I began receiving letters asking prayer for people who came from every imaginable religious creed—many of which I had never heard of before, all claiming me for their own. Fearing that my Presbyterian roof was not going to be big enough to house all these groups, while still retaining the office of elder in my own church, I affiliated myself with Rufus Jones' Wider Quaker Fellowship.

Twenty years ago when the war betweeen Fundamentalists and Modernists was at its height, many times ministers came to me and asked me to lead a crusade of some kind to unite these warring forces. "You combine all the latest discoveries that science brings to us," these men told me, "and yet you rest back upon the most fundamental of the fundamentalist concepts, such as Sacrifice and Prayer." I was deeply interested in seeing this futile war end, but I knew that I was not the man to end it. I could never forget the words of Norman Nygaard, one of my college boys, upon his return from the first World War: "We came home hungry and ready for a spiritual revival only to find the churches quarreling over the first two chapters in Genesis."

I have been called frequently to give my message in some very fundamentalist churches. I have grown to love the Fundamentalists. They go all the way with Jesus more than most of us. They consecrate themselves with more zeal. With them it is often a 100 per cent dedication. On the other hand, I am a great believer in the use of contemporaneous symbolism, that is to say, I believe that if Jesus were teaching us on earth today He would create spiritual meaning and significance in everything we experienced and did. However, to be effective, it should be simple, an outgrowth of our daily life, not something bizarre and startling.

No one can surpass Jesus' symbolism and Jesus' ritual, because it is so related to the deeper, simpler relations of life, such as eating and washing. There is the baptism with water and the spirit. There is the Blood, the most elemental basic source of life, as a means of washing our sins away. Finally there is the Cross and the Open Tomb! Simple and yet how wonderful! Why cannot we Modernists and we Fundamentalists get together, drop our civil war, and unite in a common effort to give allegiance to the spiritual conception of the universe, and make the will of God prevail!

There have been efforts to put vitality into the church from time to time that deserve thoughtful attention. One was the Unity Movement, started by Charles and Myrtle Fillmore, with the purpose of putting into the orthodox churches the faith in healing of the Christian Scientist Church without forcing anyone to leave the church. They started as Monday night groups, as an aid and adjunct to the regular church, not as a substitution, but the church spurned them, criticized them, refused to co-operate or let them co-operate with them, so they were finally forced to set up separate churches of their own. The whole New Thought Movement is thus outside the orthodox churches, and a growing rival for its memberships. Twice I have addressed the International New Thought Meetings, but always as a guest speaker.

Now we find the Oxford Group trying to instill greater drive and passion into the church but because of some of its aggressive ways it also is being scorned and avoided by many. Let us hope that it never forms a separate cult or separate church of its own.

It pains me to see every effort to deepen the spiritual life of the church be in peril of widening its already overwide divisions into separate compartments.

I have friends in all these groups. While I am aware that they all have weakness, I am also aware that they all have strength. Why cannot we stand shoulder to shoulder, each loyal to his own field, but letting the others have our friendship and our allegiance as they work in theirs?

The place where we *can* all unite is in Prayer. When it comes to talking with our Heavenly Father, "there are neither Greek or Jew, circumcision or uncircumcision, barbarian, Scythian, bondman or freeman, but we are all one in Christ."

So here I find the place to begin. The place for this union to start is in the Quiet Hour and the Prayer Groups. So I am joining in prayer and in getting my friends to pray for every sincere, earnest, consecrated program directed toward making the Kingdom of God a Reality here and now.

Service of this kind, in my opinion, should make up the largest part of the Kingdom of God Movement. The only thing that we need do, is to look after the intention, pray and prepare the ground. God will look after the harvest.

The value of this union of forces was illustrated when we united in prayer for the Preaching Mission of E. Stanley Jones in 1940-41, and again when Kagawa sent cablegrams to his friends in America as well as in other parts of the world for us all to unite in a prayer for peace.

But where the union is especially close as it is between some of us, even cablegrams are not necessary. I have often felt impelled to spend hours in prayer for some special need, only to find later that some friends, far away, sometimes in distant lands, were sending out S.O.S. calls for my spiritual support and aid. I never have a need, for instance, but Dr. Carver prays for me, and I never find a great spiritual experience but that he knows it. He on his part continually assures me that he never goes into "God's Little Workshop" with a special purpose without taking me with him in spirit.

Two of the most sympathetic contributors to this union of spiritual forces from all over the globe are Frank C. Laubach, missionary to the Moros, and Gerald Heard, missionary to the literati of the Anglo-Saxon world. Very different in temperament and mental approach they are children of the same Father in their magnificent contributions toward deepening the spiritual life of the world. One uses the intimate, friendly conversational approach to the *Personal* Christ; the other, the inner, detached meditation upon the inner *Cosmic* Christ. Then there is Starr Daily, who reaches the underworld (as well as the upper) in ways that no one on earth can match, Aldous Huxley, who reaches the young intelligentsia with incisive power, Allen Hunter, who reaches all through Love, Winfred Rhoades, Eugene Exman, Henry Hilt Crane, Paul Harris, Richard Raines, James Fremont Tittle, Richard Roberts, John Gayner Banks, Margaret Prescott Montague, Elizabeth Lee,

Grace Noll Crowell, Dan Bliss, C. R. Moseley and so on and on.

While a host of new spiritual partners have joined us since this Vision began, a number of the original list have stepped across the boundaries of Time and Space and are helping us from the Other Side. Bishop Fred Fisher of Detroit, Zona Gale of Portage, Will Boddy of Minneapolis, Brother Bryan of Birmingham, and Arthur Holt of Chicago are assisting our Vision in ways that we cannot begin to measure.

With this brief survey of the gathering of the spiritual individuals during the last few years, we are ready now to look ahead with confidence to the things that we can do in the years that are before us. We are not alone. At our side are countless thousands whose names are not found in the pages of *Who's Who* and whose incomes are not recorded in Dun and Bradstreet, but whose voices are heard in heaven above the voices of many of the leaders of the world. We must not forget that "the weapons of our warfare are not carnal, but mighty through God to the pulling down of strongholds; casting down imaginations, and every high thing that exalteth itself against the knowledge of God, and bringing into captivity every thought to the obedience of Christ."

The Replanting of the Dream

The Kingdom of God Movement is unfolding before us. We did not start it. We are not leading it. As we surrender ourselves utterly to the Christ as the Leader, and as we break down the thin barriers of partition that separate us from one another, we are doing, perhaps, all that we need to do. God will do the rest. We can be His junior partners. Only as we give over thinking of results and concentrate on seeing that we have the right intentions—intentions that are sincere, humble, loving and consecrated to the Highest—will we become true channels for this great Movement to work through us.

And this Movement, let me remind you again, shapes itself into three distinct, definite, active forms of expression:

First: the Quiet Hour for cultivating the vital experience of God in each individual heart.

Second: the Prayer Group, for cultivating the expression of vital, co-operative prayers with others.

Third: opening avenues for bringing the strength and inspiration of the Quiet Hour and of the Prayer Group into vital, constructive expression in the Social Movements of the day.

Let us take these three modes of expression and vision the tremendous possibilities contained in each.

VI. The Quiet Hour

The irresistible power for good of this Movement depends almost altogether upon the sincerity of the people associated within it upon the inner plane of Quiet Prayer and the loyalty with which they contemplate the Vision that holds us all together. There is power in the man who carries silent spaces in his being. This power becomes indescribable and immeasurable when he is linked with thousands of others who carry similar silent spaces in their souls. We are not going to ask you to go so far as to set aside an entire day for silence each week, as does the little brown man of India whose quality of stillness and whose doctrine of nonresistance shook an entire Empire from one end to the other. But we are going to ask you to emulate the example of the Man of Galilee who regularly stole away to the mountain of His soul for quiet communion with His Father before He faced the tasks and the problems of the daily round.

And what was Jesus' method of using the Quiet Hour? That is for you to interpret as best you can.

There have been so many interpretations of Jesus' method that we shall ask you to study various interpretations and select the one that brings you the closest to God.

But we all agree that Jesus did go out often in the early dawn and expose himself to the Love and Guidance of God. Just as it is the most purging, cleansing, purifying process for things in this world to be exposed to the sun's rays, so the most purging, purifying experience open to man is to expose himself for periods of complete silence, quietness, and surrender to the cleansing light of God's Love. Out of such an experience, faithfully followed day after day through weeks and months, and perhaps years, comes a cleansing of all the things that block the inflow of God's Love and Peace.

I would suggest that for the average human, the best way to start the Quiet Hour is with a period of complete relaxation and utter stillness. If one could sit for five minutes, ten or even fifteen, without tensing a muscle of the body or thinking a thought in the mind, the result would be wonderful. Not only is it a blessed experience, but it is one of the hardest to achieve. Outside the Quaker groups, certain Catholic monastic orders, and some Hindu cults, the full power and blessing of silence seems very rarely understood.

Just as that which prevents the rear feet of the hind from tracking perfectly with the front feet is usually some nervous or muscular hindrance that interferes with their perfect co-ordination, so that which prevents the perfect co-ordination of one's objective mind with the subjective mind is usually some mental or emotional hindrance which blocks the perfect adjustment between God and man. Once remove the source of conflict between the conscious and the subconscious mind so that one's surrender to God may be whole and complete, and all one's troubles are ended.

It seems silly at first glance to insist that the mere stilling of our thoughts awhile will set our thinking straight. But that is a fact. There is no more valuable training and no training more difficult to undergo than training in the stilling of our thought.

The chief conflict between our conscious and subconscious minds is caused by the inflated ego. "We are arrested growths," writes Gerald Heard. "Purgation is, then, simply the reduction of the ego. Once that swelling is reduced, the individual consciousness becomes free to develop. It becomes proficient; it can do what it wishes. With that its outlook opens up. It becomes enlightened. It is inevitable that after this it should seek the full consciousness which the saints and mystics call the Unitive state, the return to the Eternal Life."

Next to the inflated ego comes hypocrisy as the major hindrance to the spiritual life. Emma Herman wrote:

The most formidable enemy of the spiritual life, and the last to be conquered, is self-deception; and if there is a better cure for self-deception than silence, it has yet to be discovered. How many of the feverish motions rooted in the flesh and half in the nervous system which we mistake for Divine callings and inspirations would survive the test of silence? We have often been duped by some stirring of surface-feeling, or temperamental passion which clothed itself in spiritual garb, when we might have known the truth had we but taken our exaltation between our hands, as it were, and put it to the ordeal of silence.

The soul that waits in silence must learn to disentangle the voice of God from the net of other voices . . . the ghostly whisperings of the subconscious self, the luring voices of the world, the hindering voices of misguided friendship, the clamour of personal ambition and vanity, the murmur of self-will, the song of unbridled imagination, the thrilling note of religious romance. To learn to keep one's ear true in so subtle a labyrinth of spiritual sound is indeed at once a great adventure and a liberal education. One hour of such listening may give us all deeper insight into the mysteries of human nature, and a surer instinct for Divine values, than a year's hard study or external intercourse with men. That is why the great solitaries always surprise us by their acute understanding of life. They are at home among its intricacies, have plumbed both its meanness and its grandeur, and know how to touch its hidden springs of action. And they know man because they know God and have heard His voice. To know God "pre-eminently" is their distinction, and it may be ours at the cost of simple, painstaking honesty with our Maker. Prayer of positive, creative quality needs a background of silence and until we are prepared to practice this silence, we need not hope to know the power of prayer.

What remarkable Quiet Spaces this practice of silence engenders in a man; and how these Quiet Spaces when one carries them throughout the day, arise to augment the power of the Quiet Hour! It is cumulative, this practice of stillness, like a snowball growing upon itself. It is the way that saints are made. "Do thou thyself but hold thy tongue for one day," so writes Carlyle, "and on the morrow how much clearer are thy purposes, and duties; what wreck and rubbish have the mute workmen within thee swept away when intrusive noises were shut out!"

This period of silence is then a training in relaxation, in effortless motion, in selflessness, in complete self-effacement. There should be no seeking, no striving, no directed thinking whatever. There should be no striving even to see God. It is rather a resting in the presence of God, yes, in the very bosom of God, an exposing of self completely to the sunshine of God. It is marvelous how all ego can be cleansed out of one, all hypocrisy, all anger, all fears and all jealousies—they are all gone.

This brings us to the second phase of the Quiet Hour. After this ten, fifteen, even thirty minutes of purgation, we are ready to reach out and take in all that is good, beautiful and true. Reach out to the heavens and all that the heavens contain. This part of meditation is called Concentration. To hold the mind on God or your highest conception of God, on the Kingdom or your highest conception of the Kingdom, is the most marvelous training in clear thinking that could ever come to man. After weeks devoted to this religious training one finds himself growing infinitely more efficient in his everyday thinking and in all the practical affairs of life.

And what are some of the things we can "drink in" during this period of silent concentration? Three things come instantly to one's attention:

1. Pack your mind with beautiful thoughts. It is a time where the old, dead material things should be

sloughed off, and some permanent constructive visions of the true, the beautiful and the good should be allowed to go tingling through the consciousness. Such things as beautiful truths of Scripture, beautiful poems, and beautiful pictures!

2. In the second place, pack your mind with beautiful souls. It is a time to contemplate with love and trust, yes, with tenderness and adoration, those true and beautiful friends and helpers who have stood as ideals along life's pathway.

3. In the third place, pack your mind with the vision of the Carpenter of Nazareth. Read from the New Testament copiously and try to catch the spirit of Jesus, the strong, compelling motivation of that One who said, "Love thy neighbor as thyself," and "Come unto me all ye that labor and are heavy-laden and I will give you rest."

The very highest theme you can concentrate upon is your complete oneness with God. One effective way to realize this oneness is to know that in the Kingdom everything is just the opposite to what it is in this "tooth and claw" world as we ordinarily conceive it. As one rises to the Kingdom way of doing things he overcomes all obstacles, he releases whatever genius he possesses, and he creates a matrix for drawing to himself events in perfect sequence and order. To start living in heaven here and now we must contemplate Jesus' paradoxes, and glory in the marvelous release and power that they bring us: "Blessed are the meek, for they shall inherit the earth." "Turn the other cheek." "Overcome evil with good." "Love your neighbor as yourself."

As one cultivates meekness rather than pride, and love rather than power, he is prepared to see the glories of heaven all about him. Meister Eckhart wrote, " 'God is love, and he who dwells in love dwells in God and God in him.' There is a difference between spiritual things and bodily things. One spiritual thing dwells in another; but nothing bodily dwells in another. There may be water in a tub with the tub around it. But where the wood is the water is not. In this sense, no material thing dwells in another. But spiritual things dwell in each other: each several angel with all his joy and happiness is in every other angel as well as in himself, and every angel with all his joy and happiness dwells in me, and God to boot with His entire beatitude, though I discern it not."

Oneness is greater than meekness and greater than love because it requires a fusing of the two before it can come into being. When one loves another enough to wish to be ever with him, he is ready for the experience of oneness. When one is meek enough to meet and merge himself in another, his meekness is perfect. Out of this perfect meekness and perfect love is born the perfect oneness and when that oneness is with God and Christ there comes with it perfect power. Then it is that all our prayers are answered.

Jesus told His disciples in the upper room: "In that day ye shall know that I am in my Father, and ye in me, and I in you." "Abide in me and I in you." "If ye abide in me and my words abide in you, ask whatsoever ye will, and it shall be done unto you." And in His final prayer Jesus said: "Neither for these only do I pray, but for them also that believe on me through their word; that they may all be one; even as Thou, Father, art in me and I in Thee, that they also may be in us; I in them, and thou in me, that they may be perfected into one."

If you are packed enough with these beautiful things, these beautiful thoughts, this beautiful Christ, above all this beautiful oneness through Christ with the Father, you will go forth so full of good that nothing can harm you. The emptiness of evil will roll off helpless against the fullness of God and goodness within you. In the presence of danger or temptation you will be as impervious as one in a citadel.

After you have filled yourself with this fullness, then you can ask for material things. But you will not then be as insistent on receiving these things as you were at first. After you have asked for God's fullness and righteousness, all these outer things, if you really need them, will then be added unto you. When you have entered completely into this fullness of beautiful thoughts, of beautiful souls, and of the beautiful Christ, think of yourself as a beloved child of God, not as a hireling nor as an outcast. Ask simply as a child would ask for the definite things your heart desires with the simple trust that if they will be good for you, and will do no harm to others, your requests will be granted. For your Father will not give a son, when he asks for bread, a stone, nor when he asks for a fish, a scorpion.

The beginner should not use petitionary prayer too much at the start. He should rather go through the silence of purgation and the silence of enlightenment for several weeks before he tries to ask for many things. And when he does ask, he should realize that the asking merely creates the matrix and opens the door, the power has already come and the answer is already at hand in the enlightenment and union which the meditation has wrought.

And when you do ask for specific things, do so as Cinderella did, following the process she followed, knowing that if it is in accord with the Divine Plan for you, that it will be fulfilled in the right way and at the right time.

Warm your dream before the fire of a humble and loving desire. Then let the warm desire flow up the chimney of relinquishment. Then dance with your desire, if dance you must, but only with the upswinging sentiments of love, unselfishness, peace, patience, gentleness, goodness, humility and faith, knowing that the moment the dial hand begins to press down upon selfishness, hate, doubt and life's negatives it will turn into rags and tatters.

Such a dream, if properly dreamed, will ultimately find its dreamer out. You will not need to find the results; the results will find you.

VII. *Practicing the Presence*

But I do not believe that Prayer stops with the Quiet Hour. It must work itself into the muscles and the mind processes of the individual until his daily life, his conscientious application to his daily tasks, his every motion and every act reflect the peace and poise of the Quiet Hour. This is what distinguishes the Christlike prayer from all other prayers.

Beginning in the Quiet Time with the realization of your sonship with the Father, let this realization be your precious possession accompanying you every day and every hour. One need not expect to attain to this ideal in its perfection the first day. But this conception of God as our Father, all men as brothers, and Love as the Law of Life, is the conception we should strive to make into positive living realizations in our deepest, inmost souls to motivate all the actions of our lives.

After a man has combed his hair, his combed hair should accompany him all day long. After a man has composed his thoughts, his composed thoughts should accompany him all day long. Happy is he

[49]

who can carry great quiet spaces with him wherever he goes. These quiet spaces are the best shock absorbers in times of hurry and bustle and confusion. They are reservoirs of power in the dreary deserts of life, much like the oases that furnish reservoirs of life to the traveler dying of thirst. They are little spots of heaven that carry a glory and radiance with one all day long. But how can one form the habit of carrying these quiet spaces with him always?

Many people are tremendously bothered with the statement, "Pray without ceasing." They think this is impossible. They feel that it would be like putting one's mind in a vise, straining one's mind processes to the uttermost, that it would be holding one in a constant tension. It should be exactly the reverse. It is rather a relaxation and letting go, a resting in a Power greater than oneself. I have found that continuous prayer is a real possibility if it is approached in either of two ways.

First there is practicing the presence of the Christ. At the beginning the achieving of this habit will require a certain amount of very conscious attention, yes, of real mental discipline. But it will gradually grow easier and the time will come when it becomes a habit, just like practicing the art of breathing, or eating, or drinking.

Consciously think of Christ as walking at your side

to your place of work, perhaps walking hand in hand with you. Think of Him as sitting by your side in your car. If you think of Him as continuously accompanying you about your daily work, standing beside you or looking over your shoulder, hours later you may suddenly become aware that He has been standing there and assisting you all day long. He is Spirit, He is everywhere, how can He avoid being where you are? When reading a difficult book or letter ask Him to read it with you, or think of yourself as reading it to Him. If reading a Bible or very spiritual book you can think of Him as talking to you through the pages of the book.

When beginning a speech ask quickly, "Christ, speak these words through me." If facing a critical conference, ask Him to direct your thoughts and your words. When weighed down with a problem feel His hand holding you up. When evil thoughts come, exclaim, "Christ, these thoughts are not fit to discuss with Thee. Think Thy thoughts in my mind." If you are with people that you especially love, know that Christ is right in the very midst of you, for God is Love and every breath you breathe in such a gathering is shared with Christ. It is wonderful how friendships grow, how family love grows beautiful and memorable when one knows that Christ is in the center and heart of every loving group.

The last thing before retiring at night, know that Christ is standing by your bedside, guarding you, yes, standing guard over your subconscious thoughts and dreams. Because He is Spirit and because He is everywhere, ask Him to go and stand by the bedside of all those you love, especially beside all those who are calling out to you for help. Ask Him to put His hand on the fevered brow of sick ones and let His healing love embrace them into wholeness; ask Him to stand beside those who hate you, revile you, and say all manner of evil things against you, and bring them healing love and understanding. Ask Him to bring guidance and protection to your children, your brothers, to all those you hold dear, leading them by the hand in their work, in their play, in their love affairs, in their aspirations and dreams and desires.

Two booklets that will prove invaluable aids to this practice are *The Practice of the Presence of God* by Brother Lawrence, and *The Game with the Minutes* by Brother Laubach. If this exercise of the spirit interests you get these books and read them over and over. Frank Laubach's little Game which he invented of practicing Jesus' presence all day long I especially commend to you.

The other game is my invention. I call it, Living in the Kingdom. Think of the Father as the operator of a moving picture projector and of the events of life as mere films on the roll that He is reeling off for you day by day. The Operator knows what is on the reels before they are seen by you. He has arranged them in perfect sequence and perfect order, all the scenes and events coming at the right time for the perfect fulfillment of your Divine Plan. He is very loving and indulgent to His children, for while the pictures are predetermined and predestined and prearranged, He gives His children perfect free will in interfering with the process whenever and as often as they please. For instance, He allows us to take hold of the operating lever, and slow up the process, or speed it up, or (here is where we often make our worst mistakes) even to turn the pictures backward if we so desire.

He permitted the Israelites, for example, to slow up the moving pictures of their national destiny for forty years, due to their lack of faith, when, had they accepted Caleb's and Joshua's verdict and had trusted wholly in the Lord Jehovah to run the machine, they would have been inside the Promised Land in forty days. It is a long cry from forty days to forty years, and few were they who survived that wilderness march to witness the blessed day of the Lord. How many of us today have postponed our deliverance with "ultra slow motion" due to our lack of faith?

An even worse travesty, however, is to turn the moving picture *backward,* as the impatient, bitter and selfish people of the world are doing today. Many times in history we have seen this tragic blunder, and yet after thousands of years of interfering with the perfect and happy destiny of God, we still insist upon interfering with His blessed Plan. For instance, the day has come when Continents like Asia and Europe should no longer remain divided into little separate warring states, but should form some kind of large, happy and co-operative union. If they allowed the Father to turn the machine, His Union would come in the Love way, as it came in our own United States. But the Continent insists upon a king or dictator, the same mistake which we ourselves made, for four long years in the '60's; they insist upon turning the machine backward. So what do we see? Instead of witnessing brother leaning over and picking up brother from the mud, we see brother seizing brother by the throat and thrusting him down into the mud. Merely turn the machine of hate in the opposite direction from the way it is going now and this very instant we will find Love bringing every nation in the world into perfectly adjusted and harmonious relationship with every other nation, and all uniting in one great Brotherhood of Man.

[54]

While we cannot expect to get enough power into our prayer to force the *world* to come into victorious peace and harmony, we can at least start each day profoundly resolved to let the Father turn the little moving pictures in *our own* little world, that we at least might set a little blueprint among our associates of what the Kingdom of Heaven on earth *could* be if everyone would unite in living in the Kingdom of Heaven here and now.

So start the day knowing that the Father will bring every new event into your life that day with some sort of definite plan or reason, even the seemingly little trivial things, the little interruptions, disappointments, and withholdings. Know that He will bring to you just the persons that you should be with, and will keep from you the people that you should not be with; that He will send you exactly the ideas that you should have to meet the situations, and will enable you to speak them in perfect sequence and perfect order, just the right ideas to bring help and comfort and inspiration to those you are with. Know that He, if you utterly trust His handling of the movement of the pictures, will bring the supply for every need, if it be a real need, and a fulfillment to every dream in its own good time and in His own good way.

I could write a book, someday I may, on the

wonderful things that have happened to me when I do so practice living in the Kingdom. All I can do now is to say, try it, and see what wonderful joy will be yours.

Here again one cannot be visualizing a great Creator constantly turning pictures every hour and every minute of every day. But neither does one, while sitting in a moving picture house, keep his mind constantly holding the thought that there is an operator behind the scenes whose care and skill is responsible for the beautiful movement of the story before him. But every once in a while let your awareness remind you that behind the scenes is this perfect Operator, perfectly working out the pictures for your daily life.

Frank Laubach writes, "The notion that religion is dull, stupid and sleepy is abhorrent to God, for He has created infinite variety and He loves to surprise us. If you are weary of some sleepy form of devotion, probably God is as weary of it as you are. Shake out of it, and approach Him in one of the countless fresh directions. When our minds lose the edge of their zest, let us shift to another form of fellowship as we turn the dial of a radio. Every tree, every cloud, every bird, every orchestra, every child, every city, every soap bubble is alive with God to those who know His language."

Just as life becomes filled with thrills, when one practices the game of living in the presence of Christ, so life becomes filled with thrills when one begins playing the game of living in the Kingdom of Heaven.

For variety's sake I suggest that you use both methods, practicing the presence of Christ, and living constantly in the Kingdom. Practice them together, or on alternate weeks, if you desire. Each approaches the same end in slightly different ways—for both lead us along the road toward making us sons of God.

VIII. The Prayer Group

We have not begun to measure the tremendous spiritual resources available through two or three coming together and praying together. When two or three come together in perfect love, perfect harmony, perfect selflessness, so that it does not matter whether they remain silent or speak aloud their inmost thoughts, so that they can live, move and have their being as unself-consciously as though no one else were present—then indeed there is power. Such groups trace the outline of something greater than themselves; such a group creates a Master Mind and that Mind is Christ. "For where two or three are gathered together in my name," says Christ, "there am I in the midst of them."

The only way that I can conceive of making this power real to you is to compare it with the power of the Cosmic Ray. The highest discovery of science today is the Cosmic Ray. The most powerful substance, force, energy, whatever we want to call it, is the Cosmic Ray. Ordinary light rays are visible only in daylight, they function only when the sun is in sight, their power vanishes the moment the sun vanishes from sight.

In short, the various rays that are known to man are cut off or vanish very easily, and at most are available only about one-half of the twenty-four hours, whereas the Cosmic Rays are continually available, radiating their energy eternally, in sun or shade, in heat or cold, in winter or summer, in day or night, and all that is required to avail oneself of their power is to be alive upon the globe.

Having recognized the primacy of the Cosmic Ray above all other rays, let us next ask, *what is the Cosmic Ray? From whence does it come?*

This question was very hard to solve. Millikan was put to very difficult tests to discover the solution, but finally the answer came. *The Cosmic Rays come not from any one star or source of light but from the great interstellar spaces out between the stars.* In other words, out there in the Vast Somewhere—Between—the various light rays of all the suns meet and embrace in some sort of vast "cosmic orchestration," and that which is born of the meeting of the various threads of light becomes greater than the sum of all the various threads of light that unite to create it. Thus the suns, through the mere act of losing themselves and merging themselves and uniting themselves in that which is not themselves, find themselves. Out there in Space somewhere the various individual suns lose themselves and find themselves in the Universal, and in so doing, all the power is created that is necessary for producing all the life on all the planets in the universe.

Everything in the physical realm is but an outer reflection or counterfeisance of that which is in the inner realm. If all the physical life on all the planets comes from the radiation of the unseen but eternally shining Cosmic Rays radiating outward from the vast cosmic orchestration of the suns, all spiritual and mental and emotional life is coming from the radiation of the unseen, but eternally shining spiritual rays radiating outward from the vast spiritual orchestration of the Love of God.

The physical and the spiritual realms, in the past considered so far apart, are alike in this: the smaller and the more invisible a thing becomes, the more powerful it becomes. They are alike in one thing more; the more completely and harmoniously the invisible elements unite with other invisible elements, the more creative their union becomes. In other words, the more complete the integration and the more perfect the orchestration, the more irresistible is the power that is released from them.

Science does not have to believe, she *knows* this of her elements. Does *religion* know, with the same positive and living faith, this truth about *her* elements? Scientists have unwavering faith in the great laws of physical force, such as the law of gravity, the law of the tides, the law of electricity. Do religionists have the same unwavering faith in the great laws of soul force, such as the law of sacrifice, the law of humility, the law of love? In the beatitudes of the Sermon on the Mount, Jesus spoke with the confident assurance that a scientist today speaks of scientific laws. Do we share Jesus' confident assurance? Do we act upon the laws? Do we live by them? Do we conduct and control our whole lives by them?

To Jesus, Prayer was the great Cosmic Ray of the Spirit. Where two or thee come together and symphonize ("agree" comes from the word "symphonize"), asking anything in His Name, their prayers will be answered, even to the extent of lifting a mountain and casting it into the sea.

Have we churchgoers used prayer with the same scientific certainty with which the scientist uses his forces?

The outstanding thing about the Cosmic Ray is its invisibility, its selflessness, its humility, if we may use the term. These are the same characteristics of effective prayer. Jesus stated the law of the Cosmic Ray of the Spirit when He said, "Come unto me, all ye that labor and are heavy laden, and I will give you rest. Take my yoke upon you and learn of me; for I am meek and lowly in heart; and ye shall find rest unto your souls."

There was power in Jesus' prayer because He was selfless. "Not I but the Father doeth these things." And how can one become selfless? By losing oneself in the universal, in surrendering oneself to God, whom Weiman defines as the "Integrating Process of the Universe" and Matthew Arnold described as the "Great Not Ourselves" and whom Jesus described as "Our Father who art in heaven." "Take one step outside yourself," says a Persian proverb, "and you find God." Isn't that exactly the way the Cosmic Rays are produced?

How can we build Prayer Groups that will reflect some of this power of the Spiritual Cosmic Rays?

In 1935 I went to the Student Volunteer Convention at Indianapolis. My chief purpose in going was to meet Kagawa whom I had corresponded with but had never met before. When I arrived I found that a little group of praying people, inspired by a request of Kagawa for more prayer, was meeting every noon for a little period of prayer. I found where it met, and at the close of the meeting was requested to lead it each day for the rest of the convention. The next day Kagawa sent me a request to ask those present and also invite a few others that I felt sure would be "in tune" to meet with him at six o'clock New Year's morning, on the twelfth floor of the Lincoln Hotel for a special hour of prayer.

In a group where most of the people are complete strangers to each other, there is always difficulty in lifting them into that state of complete Oneness with each other and with God which we have discovered is so essential for attaining the highest levels of prayer. Because Kagawa was aware of that, I had taken special pains to gather together as far as possible people who had something in common with each other or with him.

As the word spread additional persons asked for the privilege to come and when we finally gathered at dawn that day the room was packed quite full.

The perfect selflessness and quietness of Kagawa, even his diminutive size, helped us to see not the little man of the Orient sitting there, but the Christ Himself taking the place which he in his humility had vacated. After several had prayed, and a period of silence had followed, someone asked him how he prayed. He said very simply, "I believe in praying for big things—tremendous things. I believe in taking off all limits and asking God to save entire nations, bring all of Russia to Christ." All of this was at the time of Russia closing churches, also when Italy was attacking Ethiopia. "And I believe in praying especially for big things in the way of Love. I would have us pray for Italy to love Ethiopia, for Germany to love France, for the United States to love Germany, and for Japan to love China. Let us all pray for love, more love, lots of love for the whole world."

Instantly we were swept up into a high and exalted place of Oneness with God. Forgotten was all sense of self-consciousness, of each other's presence, even of Kagawa's presence—all we could think of was Love for our fellow man, Love for God, Love for the whole world. God is Love and as we lost and merged ourselves in this godlike Love, great power like unto the power of the Cosmic Rays filled the room and we knew that God was in our midst.

After Dr. George Washington Carver spoke at the Lyceum Theatre in Minneapolis in 1937 a number of my closest friends asked if they could have the privilege of sitting in a prayer group with him on the following morning before he started back to Tuskegee. He consented to it, so I immediately picked out fifty of the clearest souls in the Twin Cities, people who frequently met with me in different capacities of prayer and who knew all the heights and depths of it. When I phoned his assistant to ask the hotel manager to indicate which room we could use for our meeting, I got word back that Dr. Carver did not want a large group—he thought I meant only six or seven carefully chosen souls who could come to his hotel room for a very quiet, intimate period of prayer.

It was now too late to call off this group. I knew the fifty would all be there at seven o'clock the next morning, and I did not want to disappoint any of them. I was conscious that Dr. Carver did not realize what deeply praying souls were in this number—clear and high enough to create the atmosphere that he felt was so essential. If people were clear and selfless enough, I knew that Dr. Carver would not care whether there were five or five hundred. What he wanted to avoid was a big crowd of curiosity seekers, such as usually plagued him for autographs and other fiddle faddle, when he went on speaking trips. So I went early to his room and asked his assistant to keep him in the bedroom end of his suite while I had someone secretly usher the crowd into the sitting room end of it, and get them all seated—mostly on the floor—before he came in. When he and I entered, I felt Dr. Carver give a little start of surprise as I led him to the two chairs prepared for us at the corner of the room.

Immediately upon being seated I said, "Let us all

be quiet for a few minutes of silent prayer." When the silence was over I spoke to him casually as though he were the only one in the room. When I ceased speaking he replied to me as simply as though we were absolutely alone, he and I and God. And we were. No one was there. I certainly was not there. Even Dr. Carver was not there. Only Christ was there. Presently Christ began speaking, using Dr. Carver's lips as His mouthpiece. And such a wonderful, such a beautiful message as we did receive! And when all present took hands at the close, forming a great interwoven circle of Oneness all over that room, closing with a couple of prayers and then a deep silence, never have I experienced a higher or a deeper or a broader and more capacious silence in all my life. As I have never met anyone who loves God more than Kagawa, I have never met anyone capable of erasing himself more completely than Dr. Carver. In their presence I have experienced the Cosmic Rays of the Spirit. In their presence I have known what Jesus meant when He said, "Where two or three agree, there am I in the midst of them."

Here was a Prayer Group which met just for this occasion, but made up of people who had met together in one way or another for years, a group that was disciplined and trained in prayer, who knew how to lose themselves in a larger group of God's children.

Again I must say, that we cannot all find Dr. Carvers to lead our Prayer Groups, but cannot we strive to learn the art of losing and merging ourselves in others? Every step we take toward humility, toward selflessness, toward transparency and incandescence is a step toward creating and releasing the power of the great Cosmic Rays of the Spirit into the world of men. Let us therefore take a big eraser and erase ourselves out of the picture, using that dear old ex-slave as our inspiration and example.

At the Isles of Shoals at the Camp Farthest Out I had the privilege of attending early morning Prayer Groups led by Muriel Lester. While she does not have the complete passionate quality of love of God that Kagawa carried with him, while she does not have the complete relaxation and release and abandonment of self as Dr. Carver has when he completely lets go (and who of us, born with our Nordic or English inhibitions, *can* emulate Dr. Carver's complete release and abandonment!), nevertheless, I have never met anyone who had such *love of people, such passionate reaching out to the suffering and needy* as has Muriel Lester. Here again the prayer circle was a circle of power.

Again let me admit that we cannot all have

Muriel Lesters to lead our devotions, but cannot we try to emulate her passionate love for suffering humanity?

In the Haverford student gatherings, there was always a Quaker quiet period that used to precede the prayer groups of Rufus Jones. While I have prayed with him alone I have never had the privilege of sitting in a prayer group with him. But I have had the next best thing to it; I have sat in prayer groups led by Jim Pinney, a former college student of mine who has become an ardent and faithful Friend and disciple of the Quaker method. In this group we sat for a solid hour in perfect silence. During the last five minutes of the period one or two spoke that which welled up in them from the inner spring. But Jim did not speak, nor did those who were highest and clearest in the circle. Out of these periods I found that all things grew settled in my mind, all problems were washed away, and there was no need to speak. When we arose, all had the same common truths uppermost in their minds. Had we spoken, it would have been wasting words. Why speak what we agree on already?

Is it possible to organize "Prayer Cells" that can generate as much power as the Cosmic Rays? It is possible if we can follow the laws of God as completely as the electrons thrown off by the celestial suns obey the laws of physics and mathematics.

In the first place, the group must possess a genuine inner harmony. This is so tremendously important that no effort should be made to carry on such a group until this is assured. Far better to limit the group to two or three rather than include one single person whose antagonism, egotism, or indifference might block the voice of the Spirit. Jesus Himself considered this so important that He frequently reduced His own twelve to three—the first little "Prayer Cell" of Christendom. But this little group generated so much power that it started forces in motion that have changed the world.

In the second place there must be complete honesty and sincerity. No pretense or false belief, no play acting or showing off can be tolerated if it is to be God's Voice that we are seeking for.

In the third place there must be a real humility, a selflessness. Not only self-conceit must be abolished, but even such a minor affair as self-consciousness. When a new group is formed containing many strangers it may take a number of meetings before all self-consciousness is eliminated.

In the fourth place, there must be some understanding of the powerful, basic laws of the Spirit; in short, a genuine sound faith built upon sound basic understanding of the spiritual laws upon which such a Prayer Group is established. For that reason an effective Prayer Group, especially if most are new to this thing, should be for half or two-thirds of each meeting period a *study* group as well.

In the fifth place, all effective prayer groups establish their routine of meeting not upon conscience and duty, but upon Love and Joy. The soul of a Prayer Group is Grace, not law. There should be sincere enthusiasm and the lilt of expectancy in every coming together. Then there is power, when the members come together who would rather pray than eat, who would rather talk and think of spiritual things than go to a dance or a movie.

Wherever there is humility there is power; wherever there is sincerity and honesty there is power; wherever there is enthusiasm and expectancy there is power. When all these elements are combined in one group there is a veritable tidal wave of power!

IX. Methods of the Prayer Group

I. Who should form these prayer groups?

1. The most spontaneous and organic selection is where a group of spiritually minded people, whose friendship has been true and tried for years, are drawn together by natural affinity.
2. Another happy arrangement is where three to six married couples who are very fond of each other and who have a sincere interest in the spiritual life come together. This is like turning a bridge club into a prayer club.
3. Another natural and easily arranged type of group is where busy housewives come together with their sewing and one reads or talks while the others ply their needles. Here we have a sewing society become a praying society.
4. Another combination is that of businessmen who wish to share their problems and find the way that Jesus would run their businesses. I have known of executives of various companies forming in this way a "Board of Spiritual Directors" to function

in problems of all the diverse businesses represented in the meetings.

5. Several very successful prayer groups have brought Jews and Catholics as well as Protestants into a common gathering. One of these groups made a special study of the background of each religion to find where they began to converge. Each member brought a prayer from his own faith that he especially loved. There was power in praying to a common God, especially when it took the simple form, which it usually did, of "God, empty us of self and fill us with Thee."

6. Another type might be called the neighborhood group. For several weeks each winter neighbors might meet in different homes for a little fellowship and prayer together. Such meetings would go far toward making the whole year a happy time for all.

In colleges the boys or girls in a dormitory sometimes gather together for a weekly or daily meeting that proves very helpful.

In a large resident hotel five or six persons met once a week and they soon found that this meeting, rain or shine, made life infinitely more pleasant and valuable.

The most effective groups are often very small; sometimes no more than three produce the greatest power. When they grow to the size of twelve, they are usually better subdivided. I have, however, known of very large groups of over fifty, functioning very successfully, but this cannot happen unless the leader is greatly inspired and is versed in some gifts and skills that few people are versed in. It might be said that the smaller the group the less technique is appropriate, and the more pure inspiration can be depended upon; the larger the group the greater the strain upon the leadership and the greater the demands both spiritually and mentally placed upon the leader.

II. *What books are effective helps for study in such a group?*

With people who are new to the discipline of deepening the prayer life, it is often well to use the first half or two-thirds of the time for study centered around some book. Merely reading aloud *The Practice of the Presence of God* by Brother Lawrence for the first half hour will do wonders in lifting a group into the attitude and spirit of true prayer. Each member might read a couple of paragraphs and occasionally, if puzzled, might ask a question or, if inspired, might make a remark. *The Song of the Souls of Men* has often been used in the early stages of a prayer group, as has also *The Lord's Prayer*, the

chapter on "The Divine Plan" being especially stimulating to prayer and thought.

Other inexpensive booklets that have been used
with value are: *The Greatest Thing in the World*
by Drummond; *Ways of Praying* by Muriel Lester;
and *Training for the Life of the Spirit* by Gerald
Heard, *For Souls Only* and *Wellsprings of Immortal-
ity* by Starr Daily. Longer books that might require several months, even a year, are: *Victorious
Living* by E. Stanley Jones or *Creative Prayer* by
Emma Herman, *A Testament of Devotion* by Kelly,
The Soul's Sincere Desire and *I Will Lift Up Mine
Eyes. The Christian's Secret of a Happy Life* by
Hanna Smith, the book that changed E. Stanley
Jones, would appeal to those of the more Funda-
mentalist attitude, and *The Creed of Christ* by Ger-
ald Heard would appeal to the philosophically
minded, and *The Sermon on the Mount* by Emmet
Fox to those who lean toward New Thought.

Other books that would prove valuable for study,
depending upon the type of groups, are: *The Meaning of Prayer* by Fosdick; *Living Religion* by Hart;
The Self You Have to Live With by Rhoades; *Fish-
ers of Men* by Clark; *Living Prayerfully* by Page;
The Inner Life by Jones; *Psychology in Service of
the Soul* by Weatherhead; *The Finished Kingdom*
by DeWater; *The Eternal Poles* by Bragdon; *God*

Helps Those by Kunkel; *The Life of the Spirit and the Life of To-day* by Underhill; *The Edinburgh Lectures* by Troward; *Impersonal Life*, anonymous; *Tertium Organum* by Uspenskiï; *Prayer and Worship* by Steere; *With Christ in the School of Prayer* by Murray; *Release* by Starr Daily and *You Are My Friends* by Frank Laubach.

III. *What methods should be used in these groups?*

During the minutes while the group is gathering there should be as little idle conversation as possible. The time should be used to relax and what conversation is necessary should be pitched on a quiet, meditative key. When the group has convened the first step to take should be to draw the thoughts of all together and bind their souls and hearts in Oneness so that the hour will be as truly spontaneous and inspired as possible. This can effectively be done by a prayer and a quiet time, followed by reading from some book.

If there is one who has had a profound spiritual experience especially one who carries great quiet spaces in his soul, the group might dispense with the reading from the book and let this one speak for ten or twelve minutes on whatever theme the spirit leads him to speak upon.

Another way is for all to repeat from memory

together some Psalm such as Psalm 23 or Psalm 121. Or have them all open their Bibles and read some passage in unison, such as Psalm 91 or Psalm 103, or Psalm 146 or the 14th chapter of John, or the 13th chapter of First Corinthians. Any of the great classical passages from the Psalms, the Proverbs, or the New Testament would serve this purpose well. Warn people not to put on the "leading" voice but to read quietly, in a low tone, and fairly slow. Do not let your own voice lead others, but trust to common sense and the rhythm in all God's children. Another way would be to ask the group to open their Bible to a chapter and all read it silently. After absorbing and pondering upon it for a silent period with the Bible still open before them, let each in turn read aloud the verse which seems to him most vital and true, and explain why.

Or one may use the hymnbook as a prayer book. Read one hymn as a prayer with a silence after each stanza. The pianist may play the chord of the last stanza and all sing, but still quietly.

Thus the first quarter or third of the hour should be used to bring the entire group into one place and into one state of consciousness, "that all might be of one mind in Christ Jesus."

The second step should be the bringing in of the individual contributions such as any experience of answered prayer in the past week, any Bible promise that served as a rock of strength, or any discovery that was of value. Then the group could go into a silence again and one by one give over their problems to God. These problems could be mentioned one by one and dropped quietly into the heart of God. As quickly as a sense of peace comes to a group they should pass on to the next problem, and then the next. Sometimes a group prefers to give these personal problems in perfect silence without even mentioning them. It is well to close the round of personal prayers by giving to the Lord each member of the group one by one. If anyone stands in special need of prayer let the silence that follows mention of his name continue a little longer.

After the personal prayers are given it is well to mention the larger problems of the world one by one, not from any prepared list, but as they spontaneously come to the mind of members of the group. If anything is omitted it may be that the need for that problem for that time is not so great. Here are some larger problems to be given over to God: graft in the great cities; capital and labor relations; racial adjustments; liquor problem; unemployment; boys in the camps; forgotten men in prisons; the underprivileged; the sick confined in hospitals; the churches; the radio and the press; the government;

our international problems; justice and peace for all nations; and finally, a prayer for a great spiritual awakening in the entire world.

Here is a detailed picture of one prayer group started by a little group of women who found release in the "Let us go deeper Movement" sponsored by the Presbyterian Church:

Over a year ago a thoughtful president of a missionary society in a great Western city felt the need now coming to the consciousness of so many to "go deeper." Intensely spiritual, she felt the call to make quest for new power in prayer. She asked a few women to an "upper room." Confessedly she had no plan, no program, but she had a need which she wanted to share.

The women came . . . an interesting group in that they were not intimate friends. But the convener had called women who might understand her own spiritual hunger. A miracle came that morning. After two hours of honest confession, of facing prayer difficulties as well as aspirations, together, the group found themselves gripped by a bond which has never been lessened.

We meet twice a month for two hours, in the morning. There has been no publicity; few know the group exists. No member is ever reminded of the meeting. Whether few or many come, it is prayer hour. . . .

The prayer hours are as nearly leaderless as possible. The convener chooses one woman to hold the very loose organization together, and to direct simply the hour of prayer. The program starts itself. Around the room each states her heart message or burden. A scope of remarkable breadth and catholicity has characterized the hours together . . . personal, church, society, national boards, unspoken requests, responsibilities and official tasks . . . whatever is the heart's need for the morning. Utter frankness and freedom, yet dignity and reserve; lack of stupid repetition and airing of troubles; sharing with perfect confidence . . . these have been characteristics. The concerns of the "upper-room" have been sacred. Never, we think, has anything been repeated outside. The matters seem not to be ours but His after we have prayed there.

Discussion is never checked, yet prayer occupies the major portion of every meeting . . . spoken prayer, silent prayer. One feels free to interrupt discussion with prayer or prayer with discussion. There is no sense of strain or "filling in" time. The two hours pass with unbelievable rapidity.

Honesty is our hobby. None wishes to claim untested faith. Conventional attitudes of belief have been discarded there. We have gone deeper to find our individual certainties. We promised never to attend from sense of duty, only from irresistible desire. Our lives were too full of trying to meet God from a sense of duty . . . here we would honestly eschew that.

So the Spirit seems to brood over our hearts. We pledge to pray for one another upon remembrance

. . . not too steadily. A sincere affection has grown up among us, and we depend more and more upon one another's prayers. I have never felt such strength from corporate prayer, never have I seen such utter sincerity, intellectual honesty, and freedom from conventional assents.

The largest, as well as one of the most successful prayer groups I ever heard of, one which, believe it or not, has continued steadily for over two years with no sign of coming to an end, might serve as a model for others of similar kind. Its long continuance is very unusual as most prayer groups are usually brought together for a limited period, a season, or at most a year. The power of this group is derived from three or four causes; first, the leader gives herself entirely to God's leading before she goes to the meeting, putting everything in His hands, even the words that she is to say. She announces that no one who holds unforgiveness toward anyone in his heart should come. Second, there are great loyalties and friendships that bind the group together. Third, the meetings are simply drenched and soaked in Scripture, one chief feature of each meeting being the memorizing of great portions of the Bible. Fourth, the leader uses unusual inspiration and skill in techniques that are effective and varied and often unexpected.

Some part of the Scriptures is memorized at every meeting. Often the members are asked at the next meeting to mention an incident during the week where the memorized passage of the past week helped them over some hard place. Long periods of silent prayer are mixed in with the memorizing. Sometimes the leader walks around among the members with an open Bible asking each to lay her hand upon it and put upon it her particular trouble. They are warned, however, that unless they are willing to *leave* it there they are not to put it there.

At every gathering some previously memorized portions of Scripture are asked for, sometimes from one person, sometimes four or more are asked to give a passage in unison, something like a verse-reading choir. Instead of listening to long testimonies repeated at every meeting, this group listens to the great promises of God and packs their minds with great passages of Scripture.

In the Black Hills of South Dakota I once saw one hundred college students come together on a hillside overlooking a beautiful mountain valley, young men and women, reticent and self-conscious in regard to things of religion, but who lost their timidity and had a great spiritual experience as they lost themselves in the presence of Nature. This was accomplished through the simple device of having them all sit and face the same direction and look upon the beautiful scene before them, forgetting that there was anyone else in their presence. First they were asked to give verses from the Bible or excerpts from poems that they especially loved. After a number of these had been given in such a way as to lift the entire consciousness of the group to a very high level of contemplation of God's beauty and majesty, they were asked to give any personal experience of finding God. No one was to look at the one speaking and no one was to pay attention to anything but God and nature. The testimony that came forth was tremendous in its spiritual power. Many lives were turned on the Upward Way.

When the groups are large, or where the people come together for temporary periods, especially where they are young and inexperienced, it is of utmost importance that all steps that are possible should be taken to remove all self-consciousness in the meditation and sharing hours.

One evening at the University of Nebraska I met with a large group of students in a woodland hut in front of an open fireplace where I witnessed a similar experience to that I had seen in the Black Hills. After my talk on prayer was finished I asked that all electric lights in the room be turned off. As the young people watched the firelight grow more dim I asked them to quote passages from the Bible, and later asked them to tell of their own deep spiritual experiences. There I saw great things happen when a group of people lost all sense of self and felt as alone with God as if they were in an inner closet with the door closed.

A "prayer laboratory" is a little different from an average prayer group. Prayer laboratories are most effectively held out in the open at summer camps. Here is a somewhat vivid, allegorical method of conducting such a group.

Ask the group to get still and become perfectly relaxed, dropping the muscular and nervous tensions first of the body, and then dropping the jealousies, hates, and fears which are merely the tensions of the mind and soul. Thus relaxed, they are ready instruments for the Father to use for His larger purposes.

Next ask them to gather together and give over to the Father all of the things in their lives that they have previously thought of as liabilities and handicaps, their fears and fantasies, their defeats and despairs, all their sins and mistakes, their disappointments, their sufferings and sorrows. Ask the group to tie these negative things together as a bundle of faggots for the fire and then place this bundle upon the altar and give it up in flame to the Lord, leaving the bundles there until all their troubles are reduced to their native nothingness, until nothing but a mere ash remains.

Tell them that they should congratulate themselves upon their sufferings and failures, yes, even upon their sins if they brought true repentance and remorse and a changed life, for the greater the abundance of material for this flame, the greater the power for carrying the good wishes and prayers to God. As Jesus found more power in the prayer of the publican who said, "God, be merciful to me, a sinner," so He finds more power in the prayer of a repentant sinner today than in that of many self-satisfied good men.

After these are gone up in flames, figuratively speaking, tell the group that upon that flame rising now like incense toward the Lord, they are to place, not the negative and bad things now, but the positive and good things—all their deep, earnest *soul's sincere desires*, and the very incense rising from their sins and failures will now have power to carry these prayers to the very throne of heaven.

After they have placed all their soul's sincere desires upon the altar and have waited till all the personal prayers have been completely taken over by the Lord, utter a prayer somewhat like the following:

"Lord, we have now given our everything: first our sins to burn away, and our sorrows to convert into joy and light; and now all our desires. We have given them so utterly and so completely to You that we have room at last for You to send us, in their place, *Your desires for us*. Enter us, therefore, O Father, and fill us with Your desires for us and for the world; let us be channels for Your great purposes, irresistible and all-powerful, to flow through us. Through us send forth Your Desire which is now our desire, that there shall be love spread all over the world, that You and Your love may be received into the hearts of all men, that justice may be done everywhere, that union and freedom may abide together on all the continents and that the Prince of Peace may rule over all nations."

Indeed, when a group is emptied of self and is witnessing the great experience of letting God pray through them the members of the group should feel a joy and a freedom that permits true inspiration to guide them as to just how that group should be conducted. I have merely indicated here in very feeble words a little of the possibilities that might come through a group, no matter how large or how small, when it is completely released into the hands of the Father.

These methods are merely suggestions. Read this

chapter over several times and jot down those methods that appeal to you, or that seem particularly fitted for your group. Then forget the list and draw out of the back of your mind whatever fits the inspiration of the moment most completely, simply and beautifully.

X. *Applying the Vision to the Nation's Needs*

Now we have reached the place where we should honestly consider just how far the power generated in the Quiet Hour of the individual and the "Orchestration Hour" of the prayer groups can manifest in the practical affairs of life.

Before a person starts upon a long journey in his auto he draws up to a filling station and sees that his tank is well filled with gas. Before we start upon this new quest let us draw up to the Scriptures and let our souls be again filled with the infinite power of God, as derived from the precious promises in His Holy Word.

And this time the verse in Scripture that I wish to bring to you is one that contains a great, dynamic power, a power that comes from the core of a great truth of God. It is so tremendous in its absolute certainty of fulfillment that it almost takes one's breath away.

Bear with me, therefore, in patience, while I try to interpret the hidden power that resides in it. The

passage that I refer to is the following: "LIFT UP
NOW THINE EYES, AND LOOK FROM THE PLACE
WHERE THOU ART NORTHWARD, AND SOUTHWARD,
AND EASTWARD, AND WESTWARD: FOR ALL THE LAND
WHICH THOU SEEST, TO THEE WILL I GIVE IT, AND
TO THY SEED FOR EVER." (Genesis 13:14, 15.)

This promise, made to Abraham by the Lord, was
kept to the last letter. This very hour the people
of Israel and of Ishmael dwell in the land which
their Father Abraham gazed upon that day. But the
promise did not begin and end with Abraham, any
more than the grapes that grew in Palestine in
Abraham's day ceased to grow after his death.

This promise is just as true today as it was then.
It applies to you and to me as effectively as it ap-
plied to Abraham four thousand years ago. For God
was here stating a universal and an eternal law. If
we examine it carefully we shall find that it contains
within it the seed of every fulfilled wish since the
dawn of history.

Therefore let us examine it closely.

FIRST: LIFT UP THINE EYES.

The initial test of every true spiritual undertaking
is the *eyes that look up*. Would you be one of the
three hundred chosen for Gideon's band? Then don't
sink your face in the water and guzzle it down, but

drink from the palm of your hand with the eyes lifted toward the horizon.

Would you be one who would have father and mother and sister and brother and houses and lands? Then don't bury your head and your heart in the selfish desire of possession, but *lift up your eyes* and "*seek first the Kingdom of Heaven*, and all these things will be added unto you."

Would you be one of the seventy chosen of Jesus to heal the sick, and cast out demons? Then don't look down at the demons and rejoice that they are subject unto you, but *lift up your eyes* and rejoice that your names are written in heaven.

In the hour of crisis look not at the poverty of your need, but at the riches of your Lord.

SECOND: LOOK FROM THE PLACE WHERE THOU ART.

What is your honest, sincere point of view when you face a problem? Don't try to stand in the place where your neighbor stands. Stand exactly in the place where *you* abide in consciousness and look from that viewpoint straight upward toward the solution and the fulfillment that God has in store for you. Every sincere, honest desire, if it be a "grown-up" desire, in other words, if it is accompanied by the upward look, which prevents it from doing violence to any moral or social code, is a prophecy of that which God in His Kingdom wishes you to have.

THIRD: LOOK NORTHWARD AND SOUTHWARD AND EASTWARD AND WESTWARD.

One day Esau came in from a hunt, tired and half famished. He smelled the pottage his brother Jacob was cooking, and all his physical nature cried out for a bowl of it to eat at once. It would have taken him half an hour to have cooked it for himself, so he asked for the pottage of his brother, who, not being so hungry, could wait and cook another mess for himself. "Give me your birthright," said Jacob, "and the pottage is yours." "I'll give you anything!" replied Esau, "anything at all to satisfy this craving in my stomach!" So Esau got his mess of pottage and Jacob got the birthright.

But Esau failed to look north or east or west. He looked only south. In other words, he let his physical desire swallow up all other values—the intellectual, the social and the spiritual. Forgotten was the value of a father's blessing, and all that it would mean to his posterity as yet unborn.

Jacob, on the other hand, looked at these things from all four directions. Esau saw only the sensory, physical satisfaction of an immediate, pressing physical need. When one is concentrated on the southern point of physical satisfaction, the values of the mind and of the soul—the values that are east and west—are forgotten.

As Esau illustrates the failure to look at all points at once, Gadski's desire to become a singer, Sarah Bernhardt's desire to become an actress, and Pavlova's desire to become a great dancer are examples of those who had a positive, constructive desire and saw it foursquare. Many a little girl has desired to become a famous actress, or singer, or dancer, who never had her desire come true because she visualized herself before a great audience bowing before its repeated ovations, with a big bouquet of flowers in her arms—and stopped there. She looked only south where all is pleasant and luxurious and full of ease. She may genuinely have loved music or dancing or the drama, which we may say is looking west. But she hated the long hours of practice, yes, the hours, months, and perhaps the years of actual patient drudgery, and apprenticeship, before she would reach the place where ovations began to come. She failed to look north and east. The difference between the average little girl and the Pavlova and the Bernhardt and the Gadski, is that one sees only a part of the price that one must pay, and the other sees all of it, and *loves it all*. Not until a person sees all of what he is looking for and loves all of it can he be said to be looking north and south and east and west.

Having seen all of that which you vision, the northward as well as the southward parts, the hard as well as the easy parts, the inner as well as the outer parts, the question you should ask yourself is; Do I love all of it, the hard, the easy, the inner and the outer? If you still do, the land is yours.

Now, seeing a thing in one's heart means to see it with the heart of love. That which you love, loves you. If you see little children with the heart of love, children will love you and come to you. If you look at little dogs with the heart of love, little dogs will come to you and follow you around. If you look at beautiful ideas with love, they will come and be yours. If you look at a land with the heart of love, that land will be drawn in love to you and will belong to you. A man who sees the pictures in an art gallery and loves them, really possesses them from that time on. The art gallery attendants merely take care of them for him, the art gallery houses them for him, but he is in truth the real owner of them, and that without the necessity of paying rent for their housing or paying wages for their care and protection. Does his ownership of the art gallery impoverish the art gallery? No, it enriches it. And it is for this ownership which enriches what it owns that all art galleries were built. For this love element is not to be confused with cupidity and covetousness. This love is just the opposite of these qualities —even as unselfishness is the opposite of selfishness.

If the heart lens of the field glass with which you see the land you are to possess leads you to love it, then the mind lens leads you to see yourself living in the midst of the plenty of the land and enjoying it. *Loving* and *visioning* constitute the bifocal way of seeing that which God has ordained to be yours.

FOURTH: THE LAW OF VERIFICATION.

Out of the mouths of two witnesses comes perfect verification. If God is in this "witnessing" then the verification is indeed complete.

Here is where we can bring to our aid another great promise from Scripture, this time not from the "old" but from the "new covenant" to support, sustain and cross-fertilize the great message of the first promise.

Jesus stated this law twice, once in its active and once in its passive form. "Where two or three are gathered together in My Name there I am in the midst of them." "If two of you shall agree on earth touching anything you shall ask, in My Name, it shall be done for them by My Father which is in Heaven."

[93]

So the next step is to find, if possible, a few kindred souls and tune in with them to the same vision.

FIFTH: THE LAW OF RELINQUISHMENT.

Having taken the vision and breathed wholeness into it, by seeing it northward and eastward and southward and westward, and having found a brother who sees it likewise with you, *the next step is to give it to God and go off and forget it.*

The farmer first gathers the seed in his hand, sees that it is whole and flawless, and is filled with the life-giving germ of growth, and then plants it and goes off and leaves it. He does not continually dig it up to see whether it is growing. He *knows* it is growing. He gives himself wholeheartedly to other concerns while this seed rests deeply and functions gloriously in the deep soil of God's Love. Likewise, when you have visioned the land completely and given it to God, your work is done. It is now time to go away and rest awhile in doing the Lord's business, while He does yours.

An outstanding characteristic of Abraham's *seeing*, greater than that of any other man's in history, was his willingness to give back to God the things which he had seen so clearly and loved so dearly, whenever God called. Abraham would have given his son Isaac back upon the altar of the Lord, had not

God intervened to tell him that a faith and a trust and a surrender so great, proved that he was deserving not only of keeping his son, but through him of being the Father of a great race whose numbers would be like the stars in the heavens and as the grains of sand upon the seashore.

Having seen the country in its completeness, northward and southward, eastward and westward, the inner and the outer, the hard and the easy, if you love it, and can still give it to God, then the land surely and truly is yours. For nothing insures one the rightful possession of a thing, so much as the willingness, if God wills it, to give it away. This was the test met by the mother of the babe which Solomon offered to have cut in half, one half to go to one who claimed to be the mother, and the other half to the other. The false mother would have acquiesced in this division before she gave up her claim; the true mother would have been willing to surrender her child, even to another, in order that the child might live.

II.

When the great depression of 1929 burst upon this country, fifty thousand people out of a population of 450,000 in the city of Minneapolis were thrown out of employment. By the end of the second winter the surplus funds of the city were exhausted. The community chest was empty. People who had given to the breaking point would not be able to give as generously another year. Little nest eggs saved up for a rainy day had vanished. Insurance policies, kept up until now for borrowing purposes, had lapsed. Little mortgages, now grown to great ones, were wiping away houses and lands. The whole city had been bled white by two exhausting winters of depression and would not be able to meet the situation ahead unless some new solution presented itself.

Now was the time of all times, as far as Minneapolis was concerned, for someone to catch a vision of God. So I decided that the time had come for someone to make use of the Great Discovery that I have just described.

I. WE LIFT UP OUR EYES.

First of all I went into my closet and *lifted up my eyes* to the great God who has never failed His children in carrying into fulfillment every promise He ever made—when they truly call upon Him in perfect humility and perfect trust.

For days I gave this need prayerfully to God. I knew that somewhere, somehow, there must be a method of taking care of the unemployed in this great city, if God would just open our eyes to it. After many weeks light began to come.

II. FROM THE PLACE WHERE WE STOOD.

But the biggest task of all was looking the problem itself straight in the face from all the angles of *north and south and east and west*, and this part of the process, let me remark, is where something besides cloistered prayer is necessary. Here is where the prayer process must put on overalls and plow and dig and delve. Here is the point where Edison's definition of genius (which is nothing but prayer in action) is right: "Inspiration is 99 per cent perspiration."

I dug, I delved, I perspired. I studied into the statistics available for the unemployed in Minneapolis. I asked people who ought to know, what was the likelihood of the city government's being able to meet the situation in the coming winter, or of the charity organizations' ability to meet it.

Then I began an investigation of methods being used in other cities—the trade and barter schemes that seemed feasible, the script method, etc.

Finally I prepared a more or less definite but tentative plan that seemed to contain the germ of the solution provided it had the right man to head it, and the support and co-operation of the city government, and the prayers and moral support of the churches and religious people behind it.

I even picked the actual man who would be competent to head this whole project. I had a half-day conference with him and he promised to be on hand at a meeting in the mayor's office—but I am getting ahead of my story.

IV. Two or Three Agree Together.

I was now ready for the hazardous step of sharing this dream with others and getting them to "agree" in visioning it together with me. I began this gradually with one or two kindred souls, and then when it had safely weathered this "exposure" without damaging "explosions" or "leakages" or "cold blanketing," I presented it to the entire "Board of Spiritual Directors." After they had "agreed together" that the plan was a good one, I acted upon their urging and together we met with the Mayor of Minneapolis and his secretary one Sunday afternoon to look the whole matter over together.

When the Sunday afternoon arrived, all things went as expected except one. The man we had selected as the one most capable of heading the project did not appear. We accepted that as God's way of telling us in His gentle manner that he was not the man God had chosen for the task. Therefore we trusted that He must be choosing another, another with exactly the same amount of executive and organizing genius as the one who failed to come.

The Mayor, although a praying man, was not accustomed to seeing dreams presented so candidly in his office, nor was he accustomed to meeting people who believed that dreams come true. While he could offer no help he offered no obstructions and the meeting finally ended with a fine spirit of fraternal co-operation.

V. WE PLANT THE VISION.

The project up to this time, you will realize, had been limited entirely to the realm of the unseen. It was not even visible as yet to the outer eye. Not even a leader had come into view, much less the workers. All was in the realm of amorphous half-light. It was a mere looking to God from the place where we stood, a mere looking northward, and southward, and eastward, and westward, a mere agreeing together of two or three. We had reached the stage where the next step in the divine unfoldment was to take the whole dream, the whole prayer, the whole plan—whatever you wish to call it—out into the garden of God and plant it. Yes, plant it and go off and forget it.

It so happened that a number of us had gone to a

camp which we called "The Camp Farthest Out," a retreat for experiencing the wholeness of the spiritual life. This camp was to last for three weeks. There we took up the project of organizing the unemployed as the chief topic of an entire morning's discussion and with uplifted eyes together we saw God's workmanship in this plan. And great was the sense of peace and power that came to us in the final hour which was an hour of prayer and silence, when we planted our dream in the heart of God.

VI. THE VISION FINDS FULFILLMENT.

The next week we began to read in the Minneapolis *Journal* of a perfect replica of our vision for the handling of the unemployed for the coming winter. But it was in the words and functioning of another man, a man we had not thought of in this connection at all, but a man who in character and capacity was as ideally fitted for organizing and carrying on such an endeavor as the one we had originally considered to head up the project. Moreover, this man not only had the character and the capacity, but he was fired with the vision.

You may recall how the Disciples tried to select a successor to Judas. In order to give God a part in the selection they sifted the candidates down to two and then drew lots trusting God would preside over the drawing. In short, they did the nominating and let God do the electing. They forgot that God likes to do the nominating as well as the electing. Had they lifted their eyes and looked north and south and east and west, they would have seen God choosing Saul of Tarsus, not by lot, but by lightning.

During all the time we had been looking at the problem northward, southward, eastward and westward, God had been selecting the man to direct our vision. He had sent this man across the continent on a passionate errand, getting data on how other cities were trying to solve their unemployment problem. He was returning from this trip asking himself over and over again, "Who is the man who should do this thing for Minneapolis?" While we were praying for God to send us the right leader, he was crossing the state of Wisconsin, when suddenly a question hit him squarely between the eyes, "Why don't *you* do it."

So upon his return he immediately set about it and everything fell into his hands as though it had been prepared ahead of time for him—as it actually had been.

What followed I hardly dare to put in print for the general reader, for it would test the credulity of any one. Even before this man knew of our interest in his project he drew leaders from our group, he established a partnership of prayer with us, and we saw our mutual dream come into fulfillment in a marvelous way before our very eyes.

I haven't time or space here to enumerate the great quantity and variety of service the "Organized Unemployed, Inc." of Minneapolis rendered to the thirty thousand unemployed who registered in it.

Thousands were helped in legal service, thousands more were saved from mortgage foreclosures, and still more thousands were aided in medical and first aid service. Twenty thousand articles of clothing were renovated the first year, and made over as good as new; twelve thousand pairs of shoes were remodeled; thirty-three thousand yards of new cloth were made into clothes; six hundred thousand meals were served for scrip; labor and material were traded for 156,000 bushels of farm produce from 218 farms; 8,500 cords of wood were cut in 37 wood camps. Farm products going to waste on farms for want of market were traded for the labor of harvesting them, these articles were canned and bottled and served the hungry tables of thousands of unemployed in Minneapolis during the winter months.

Thousands were given regular employment, thousands more part-time employment, and the whole city and surrounding country felt alleviation of the unbearable strain of want and misery which had been settling like a pall upon the city. Before the first year was over the success of the movement became known all over the world, and thousands of people seeking the solution to their own local problems came to study its workings as pilgrims journey to a shrine.

Over 205,000 main line telephone calls and several thousand general inquiries by mail came in from all over the United States and Canada, and Europe. A week did not pass that did not see delegations from all over the country and even from Canada and England visiting the plant. Newspapers and magazines everywhere told the story of this Minneapolis Movement, including the *Literary Digest* (January 4, 1933); *Good Housekeeping* (March, 1933); *The Farmer's Wife* (April, 1933); the *New Outlook* (December, 1932); the *Christian Advocate* (N. W., January, 1933); *The Jewish Forward; Zion's Herald; The Broadcaster; Commercial West;* the *Commonweal,* New York City (Catholic); *The New York Times;* the *Christian Science Monitor;* and hundreds of other newspapers, in addition to thousands of syndicated articles through the Associated Press and the United Press, which carried long articles about it.

We can sum up the above by saying that this project which began as a dream no larger than a mustard seed, became a towering tree and the birds from near and far came to rest in its branches.

HERE THEN WAS CONVINCING PROOF THAT WHEN

TWO OR THREE VISION A PROJECT TOGETHER IN
THE SPIRIT OF LOVE AND HARMONY, EVEN WHEN
THEIR VISIONS DO NOT AGREE IN ALL DETAILS, THE
FULFILLMENT OF THEIR COLLECTIVE PRAYER IS BET-
TER THAN ANY OF THE INDIVIDUAL VISIONS.

And that leads us to a very significant and far-
reaching truth:

IF GOD CAN TAKE OUR LITTLE VISIONS WHICH
TWO OR THREE GIVE TO HIM IN THE SPIRIT OF HAR-
MONY AND LOVE, AND BRING FULFILLMENT GREATER
THAN ANY OF US ALONE CAN DREAM, WHY CANNOT
WE USE THE SAME METHOD IN GIVING GOD OUR
LARGER VISIONS FOR THE SOLUTIONS OF OUR NA-
TIONAL AND WORLD PROBLEMS IN THE SAME SPIRIT
AND WITH THE SAME FAITH, TRUSTING HIM TO CRE-
ATE OUT OF THE VERY IMPERFECTIONS IN OUR
VISIONS THE GREAT PERFECTION OF HIS LARGER
PLAN!

If you do not believe this, you should lay this book
aside at this point and go no farther. *But if you do
believe it, turn to the next chapter and read it
through* carefully from beginning to end. Just where
does your vision and viewpoint agree and merge with
the rest of ours in this great Orchestra of Love?

XI. Vision of a Christian Economy

You are now ready to listen to one of the most audacious proposals ever made by anyone. It is that you and I, and those others that we can get to agree with us, undertake to see the coming of a perfect social order by the simple act of lifting our eyes, and looking from where we are, northward and southward and eastward and westward, with the positive assurance down deep in our hearts, that the land of happiness and harmony and abundance which we shall thus see together, will be given to us. Indeed, can there be a more daring or audacious act than the simple act of laying hold of the promises of God!

Permanent things do not start in the market place with hubbub and sounding of trumpets. They begin on the mountaintop in secretness and stillness, in fasting and prayer. The more things we do, from the outside only, are just so many things that we have to do over again. We tried to make the world safe for democracy by the blare of trumpets and the roar of cannon, only to find that all this work had to be done over again. We have seen prosperity grow in this nation to the tune of high-pressure salesmanship and ballyhoo, up until 1929, only to find after that date seventy per cent of our industries operating at a loss, millions of people forced from farms because of tax and mortgage foreclosures, five hundred thousand lawyers, doctors, and dentists forced to close their offices because people could not pay for their services, and ten million heads of families, together with their dependents, numbering over one-third of the entire population of this country, wholly dependent upon charity for their lives; while banditry, divorces, desertions, suicides, kidnapings, murders, and strikes increased until we had a situation almost as bad as open warfare.

Yes, everything that we have done from the outside we have had to do over again. Only things that start from the inner seed, grow straight and true and last forever. Things that grow from the husk do not grow at all, or if they do grow, they grow crooked. The trouble with the world has been that it has trusted too much to the crooked process of righting wrongs. You remember the crooked man who jumped into a bramble bush and scratched out both his eyes. Then he jumped in again and scratched them in again. But when they came in again they were still crooked. You may remember also how, by means of jumping into the ballot box, we attempted to scratch out liquor, and then jumped back into the same bramble of legal processes to scratch it in again. And there is no question that liquor is just as crooked, if not a little more so, now than when we scratched it out. We shall never solve the liquor problem in this nation, or in any nation, nor shall we solve any other problem that faces us, as long as we trust to the bramble bush formula. The only way to solve our problems permanently is through the seed formula. In other words, the place for this nation to begin, if it really wishes to solve a problem, is to get a vision.

Great things are done when men and mountains meet,
They are not done by jostling in the street.

Greater than the power wielded by the Brain Trust is the power that could be wielded by a "Spiritual Trust." Hidden deep in this book is the prayer that an ever-growing band of Gideons of the Spirit made up of "old men who dream dreams and young men who see visions," will co-operate together in seeing with eyes of faith a VISION OF GOD'S PERFECT PLAN FOR THE NATION WE LOVE.

I. LET US LIFT UP OUR EYES.

We have now come to the place where we must recruit our *Gideon's Band* for this *Vision of Today*. Will you be one of them? Remember the chief test

[107]

you will have to pass if you qualify for the chosen army is: Can you drink from the River Jordan with your eyes lifted and your heads up? If only 300 qualify that will be enough. If 300,000 can pass the test it will be still better. If 3,000,000—but why scan the horizon for numbers? Can we count on *you*? Remember that "one with God is a majority."

In this band we shall need only those who believe in the power of a vision. We especially need those who realize that the quieter and more still we grow with God the more powerful and irresistible our vision will become, and that this vision that grows from within, like a seed, has elements of strength and elements of permanence in it that no organization made by man has power to resist.

"In the beginning God." That is the way the Bible begins. It is the way everything should begin. Now, having begun at the right place we are ready for the next step.

II. Look from the Place Where We Are.

The vision that we are holding together depends for its power and usefulness not upon the lock step, but the free step; not upon regimentation, but upon orchestration. It blends the various movements for which each is best adapted into a beautiful tapestry of Love and Harmony.

Vision of a Christian Economy

Probably the greatest *a cappella* choir in the world is that of my own neighbor college, St. Olaf. In this choir the great director does not require that all sing soprano, or that all sing bass, or that all sing tenor. He insists that each one find out his or her own voice register and then he tells each to sing "from the place where thou art." There is a man in this choir who can sing a whole octave deeper than any other bass in the world, I understand. Suppose this man admired Caruso more than any other singer he had ever heard, and therefore wished to be allowed to sing tenor in the choir. Imagine the discord that such an attempt would cause. In the same way you will cause nothing but discord and raucous notes if you hypocritically pretend to believe something you don't believe, and try to contribute some other vision than the actual vision you see and feel at the place "where thou art."

That means that if you are a radical you are to vision your radical Utopia to the best of your ability, and if you are a conservative, you are to vision your conservative Utopia to the finest and clearest heights you can conceive. In fact, the clearer you are in your individual vision, the greater help you will be to the general group, providing that where all these converging viewpoints meet is in the "lifting up of thine eyes" toward God.

As the choir achieves its unity of effect, not by making all the voices alike, but by requiring that all the singers look in the same direction—keep their eyes fixed upon one point—the baton of the director —so our unity of effect will be created by one thing, by keeping all of our eyes turned in the same direction—toward God. And just as the singers agree that the power residing in the director is the *one power* that all *must* obey, so the more completely we, in this group of spiritual orchestration, can trust implicitly in the *one unifying power of God as the center of all good,* the more completely, the more quickly, and the more perfectly the Utopia which we all would love to see will come to pass.

III. LOOK NORTHWARD AND SOUTHWARD AND EASTWARD AND WESTWARD.

Unless the redeemed society which you see from the place "where thou art" has a place for every individual in the country, rich and poor alike, and unless your social order provides for all to have some opportunity for self-expression along lines that Nature and God has shaped for them, then your plan will not harmonize with ours. But unless you have looked north, which means you are fair to the rich, and unless you have looked south, which means you are fair to the poor, and unless you have looked east, which means you have taken into consideration the needs and rights of other nations, and unless you have looked west, which means you have taken into consideration the needs and rights of future generations, and finally, unless you look up and give your vision in its entirety to God—then you have not done *your* part toward making this prophecy come true. But if you have met all these conditions, then you can rest in perfect quietness and in perfect calmness, knowing that your vision will come to pass and that nothing can prevent its coming to pass.

IV. Two or Three Agree Together.

A bee hunter, seeking the source of wild honey, does not catch only one bee, and let it loose in order to follow its trail. He catches four or five and traces each to its destination. He goes northward a way and lets one loose. It rises into the air, circles around a few times as it seeks to find its bearings, and then goes off on a "bee line" for the hive. Then he goes southward a ways and lets another one go. Likewise he sends one from the east and one from the west. Each makes a "bee line" for its hive. Then he traces out where these four "bee lines" meet, and, sure enough, there is where the honey is to be found.

Suppose now we gather together four persons,

each representing different points of view, all having visions of an economic and social Utopia for our nation and all making "bee lines" from the place where they are, toward that Utopia they dream of. Where these lines meet the Utopia will appear.

"Where one dreams a dream it remains a dream; where two dream a dream it is a vision."

Samuel and John Adams visioned independence for the colonies but it was not until little groups of "Minute Men" visioned it with them that it came to pass. Gideon caught a dream in a threshing floor but not until he had three hundred carefully selected men capable of cherishing the vision deeply in their hearts was the liberation of the Israelites from the Midianites possible.

So the next step that awaits us is to find the three hundred sons of Gideon, and let these three hundred expand into three hundred thousand "Minute Men," and these in turn expand until they and their vision fill the nation; then we may expect the great spiritual and social regeneration of America to take place and a truly spiritual and harmonious social order come to pass.

In this spirit of consecration to a cause greater than ourselves, and of devotion to a vision almost as high as heaven itself, let us join our song to the great celestial choir and see what harmonies, un-dreamed of, shall come forth.

With this spirit of unity and agreement, by bring-ing the diverse and individualized elements in our individual separate viewpoints into powerful har-mony through *lifting up our eyes* toward the great Director of the chorus we are ready to take the next and final step toward bringing our Vision into fruitage when the time of harvest has come.

Before we attempt this orchestration let us real-ize clearly that this entire economic problem is not necessarily such a materialistic thing as many pre-suppose, but is essentially a very spiritual thing. In the larger sense, the spiritual and the material values —when in proper alignment, which means when first things are placed first—are amazingly one. Just as vapor when cooled or condensed becomes water, and water in turn when cooled becomes ice, so that in-tangible element called the spiritual substance of God when sufficiently cooled or condensed through contact with the practical needs of man can actually find expression in such material things as money. As vapor can be condensed down to solids, so all true spirituality, if it truly be spiritual, must find ex-pression sooner or later in works, deeds, substance. "By their works ye shall know them." "By their fruit ye shall know them." These were some of the revealing words of Jesus.

But while money can be a spiritual thing and serve as a means to spiritual enrichment, we must not forget that it can also become a temptation to misuse. There is probably no other thing that has caused more hate, more wars, more human sufferings between families, between nations, between races, than the scramble for the almighty dollar and the comforts and privileges that adhere thereto. Truly the Bible was right when it said, "The love of money is the root of all evil."

While Jesus said that if we seek *first* the Kingdom of God and His righteousness, all these things would be added unto us, He implied that the final goal for a man or a nation should not be wealth, nor even well-being, and security—but a good soul. "What shall it profit a man if he gain the whole world and lose his soul?" Let us keep that central as our vision grows. In what ways can our economic system meet the material needs of man so as to contribute toward and not retard the developing in him of a good Soul?

Following close on this as in natural sequence, let us realize that one of the best ways to keep money spiritual, a contributing and not a retarding factor in the development of a good Soul, is to keep

it as fluid and flowing and vaporlike as possible.
In other words, too much grasping and greed and
miserliness destroy prosperity rather than promote
it. Banks bursting with gold, barns bursting with
grain, storehouses loaded with cotton are more a
menace to prosperity than an aid. A tithing habit
is one way of preventing the fine vapor of one's
spirit from becoming chilled and hardened into the
ice of complacency, selfishness and materialism
This realization came to me with renewed force whe
I crossed the Mississippi River this winter between
Minneapolis and Saint Paul and beheld the river a,
open and "unfrozen" in February as it is in June
caused by the fact that the Ford dam farther dow
was open for a steady flow to turn the wheels of
the factory. That tiny, steady, controlled flow, small
as it was, was sufficient to keep the mighty Mississippi between the two cities in an open, fluid, flowing
state when all the ten thousand lakes without such
outlets were frozen sheets of ice.

We have a right to seek some security, but remember that looking after our own individual security while millions of others are exposed to all
the chances of fate is not only mocking God but is
ultimately ineffective as a way to security. We need
warmth, shelter, clothing—yes—but so do millions
of others. Those who have too much have been blind

to the imperative needs of others and to the great possibilities for supplying them. The tension lies between the planning abilities of those having too much on the one hand, and the neglected needs of those having too little on the other.

Let us now take the final step consciously, thoughtfully, and wisely. The trend has been away from the robber-baron ideal to the ideal of social responsibility —from selfish individualism toward co-operation and, where needed, toward socialization. We have been gradually but steadily moving toward the ideal of the brother's keeper. Let us be careful to stop the pendulum in the middle and not let it swing to the other extreme as it has done in some unfortunate countries.

And there is no reason why we should not believe that the time has now come for us to take a prodigious forward step toward the fulfillment of that ideal. The most significant thing about the pace of material progress of the last hundred years has been its remarkable *acceleration*. Henry Adams stated, and it has never been disputed, that every ten years the acceleration of progress has been equal to the hundred years prior to it. At this ratio of spiral speeding up the next ten years should witness an advance beyond the dreams of man. It is partly our failure to adjust ourselves to this rapid spiraling which has brought on the jars of the present day. Fascism and Nazism and Communism were sporadic attempts on a materialistic plane to channel this mighty flooding force; they show that man's spiritual growth has not yet caught up with his materialistic progress.

With this much agreed upon at the outset we ought to expect some remarkable harmony in our orchestration of the economic picture. But this can only be possible if we remember that the Bass and Tenor voices blend beautifully when the owners of the voices *sing*, but they clash frightfully when the owners *yell*. If the Bass should suddenly roar that the Baritones were all communists and if the Tenor should shriek that the Basses were all grafters we would have an excellent *riot*—but no chorus. We have tried the riot method so often in our "Economic Symphonies" in the past, why not try the chorus method for once? And when the singing begins, let us listen, not for discords, but for harmonies. Let us hear the Bass singing of veneration, initiative and steadfastness, the Baritone singing of compassion, equality and security, the First Tenor singing of sacrifice, service, and brotherhood, and the Second Tenor singing of progress, balance and permanence. We all want all these things; we differ only in the matter of the proportion. Let us be still together and let God help us determine the proportion.

Finally, let us remember that out of contrasting opposites, when they approach each other in the spirit of harmony, all the great things of the world have come. Some call this the law of Polarization; some call it the law of Love. Out of the harmonious blending of frigid cold and torrid heat comes our most heavenly weather. Out of the marriage of the most masculine of men and of the most feminine of women is born a son who surpasses both his parents. So in this atmosphere of contrasting viewpoints when tolerance and understanding bridge the gaps that lie between, let our deepest Bass and our highest Tenor meet and blend and bring forth the greatest music this old world has ever heard.

Then, remembering that the most important law of the choir and the orchestra is to keep your eyes upon the director, let us proceed to the "Orchestration of our Vision."

The Bass

First comes the Conservative Individualist who believes that the objective of the ideal Social Economy is to protect private property and the individual freedom of initiative. The methods advanced would be to return to the proven system of free competition, a balanced budget, and the traditional American system, because it has proved effective for stimulating invention, increasing production, encouraging originality and initiative, and has increased the standard of living more than five fold in the last hundred years. Our Bass singer holds the viewpoint that it is not the system but the greed and selfishness that enters into any system that brings the evils to the social order. Therefore he favors holding fast to all that is good in the old method, and making only the minimum changes necessary to protect the values of "rugged" individualism from the evils of "ruthless" individualism.

He would begin his reform by ending the extravagances in government, which maintains a dozen political jobs and salaries where one would be enough, a system that abounds in duplications and inefficiencies, that supports a medieval organization of multitudinous county governments, fifty in a state where five would suffice. For cities he favors the City Manager Plan.

He favors a great reduction, if not complete ending, of all crippling taxes on industry, including the income tax, and imposing, instead, one comprehensive inheritance tax. He holds that it is socially and economically unwise to restrict personal initiative in any way, and the curbing of acquisitiveness should be all done at one time, at the end, not at a thousand points along the way.

He would end the problem of unemployment by means of three definite safeguards: first, complete abolition of child labor; second, abolition of old age labor by adequate pensions; and third, progressive, but not over-hasty shortening of the hours of labor. He would recognize the necessity of planning our own economy with an eye to its proper relationship and open co-operation with the economy of other nations. He would recommend the gradual and re-ciprocal lowering of trade barriers and the formation of economic unions, such as Otto T. Mallery suggests in *Economic Union and Durable Peace*,* and a new realization that a rich nation has no right to roll in plenty while other nations starve or suffer through inadequate access to raw material markets of the world.

He would urge leaders of industry to get a higher

* Such men assert that a rich nation cannot remain rich while other nations are impoverished by lack of access to raw materials and to the trade of the world. They assert that when France put up trade barriers in Indo-China which let in only one-sixty-eighth as much trade from Japan as from France, the attack on Indo-China was invited. They indicate that when Britain gave such preferences to British goods in Malaya that Japan could get over the barriers only $1.00 for every $110.00 of British goods, it was prudent to put the strongest fortress at Singapore in Malaya. They point out that soldiers will cross frontiers if goods cannot do so. This reveals how an adequate solution of our economic problem will contribute much toward achieving a permanent peace.

ideal of stewardship and trusteeship, and he would urge all schools, churches and homes to foster in their children higher ideals of public service and responsibility.

The Baritone

In contrast to the rugged individualism of the Bass stands the radical socialism of the Baritone. Here the objective is the full employment of the man power of the nation through the socialization of all industry that can be socialized, with production for use, not for private profit. With everyone working, and no idle hands, with the present efficient machinery available for production, an abundance could be produced that would enable all families to live in abundance and no one ever to be in want.

Each child would be educated until he was twenty-five, and each person upon reaching the age of sixty would receive an adequate pension, with the privilege of devoting the rest of his life to study or travel, or to the hobbies he loves. As fast as the productive power of the nation increases under the continuous stream of improved machinery and labor-saving devices, the purchasing power of each individual will be increased to the full measure of the abundance produced each year by the nation.

The Baritone believes that once this system is put

into operation with modern machinery creating wealth from unlimited national resources, and everyone working and no idle hands, we would find the purchasing power of each person would double and triple what it is now, and each would enjoy long vacations each year, and no one would need to work after he was fifty-five or sixty unless he chose.

By putting an end to the ever recurrent overproduction and under pay of the past he would promise an end to the recurring periods of boom and depression. He feels he would be rendering a spiritual value to the nation by putting an end to the major inequalities in income and thus abolishing the cause of such crimes as burglary, kidnaping, blackmail, etc. As crime is our nation's greatest waste, costing us fifteen billion dollars every year, its decrease would add greatly to our true national prosperity.

The Tenor

The Tenor believes that the way to change society is for the individual to change his own soul. He believes no discipline can take the place of self-discipline. He would change society by changing himself with his emphasis placed almost entirely upon the spiritual change—with or without changing of the economic basis of society as a whole. He places his trust so completely in the free flow of the inner spirit, for instance, that he is willing to give up houses and lands, indeed, security of all kind, and live as Saint Francis lived, letting the needs of the morrow take care of themselves. Without wallet, extra shoes, or ballast of any kind, such a one moves through life trusting to the power of the Spirit as being adequate to take care of all the needs of the body; he is armed with sufficient fortitude to wait upon the Lord, or even to do without, if the Lord so wills. Muriel Lester, Mahatma Gandhi and George Washington Carver have lived largely that way; George Mueller began his Bristol Orphanages entirely on faith. In each of these cases God's provision has been adequate to all their needs. This is undoubtedly the most idealistic method—the method most closely approximating the way we shall all conduct ourselves in heaven some day—the method which, if sincerely entered into by all people all over the world, would probably bring to earth a veritable Kingdom of Heaven. But for that very reason—because so few of us are worthy or ready for the Kingdom of Heaven now—it is the section of the choir which will have the fewest singers. But while they are only a handful, nevertheless, because of the soul force they express, their song may rise with the greatest power of all.

The more practical forms such singers take are

the forms of communal living together. The Consumers Co-operatives in its highest and most unselfish, spiritual forms represents probably the most practical, external, tangible expression of this idealism. But the form is not the essential thing in this group. It is the spirit, and once attain the spirit of trust and unselfishness in sufficient degree through means of disciplines, no matter how severe, the spirit will create its own essential forms adequate to the needs of the hour.

The Second Tenor

The Second Tenor represents the idealistic conservative with emphasis upon the good of all mankind. He is in sympathy with the spiritual disciplines of the individual as expressed through Saint Francis, but he doesn't want to stop with the individual. His objective is to reconstruct our society in all its phases so as to produce a better and happier race in this and future generations. The method proposed to achieve this end is to begin with all that has been proven good, useful and effective in our traditional system of free enterprise and private property, study all points of view for objectives that lead toward a better people, and select those that blend and are attainable. He proposes to redesign our economics, our government, even our religious forms, in such a way as to produce a better race in the future while preserving a maximum of freedom and happiness for the present generation. He would make changes only where an improved result seems assured for the benefit of *all* the people, and considers quality as well as quantity, both in material goods and in future population. He would entrust responsibilities for vision and leadership to a concentration of best minds.

This opens on vast areas. Idealistic means of carrying on society while putting into operation projects for improving the race now and in the time to come would fill as many books as might be required for the Tenor group to show the steps necessary to improve the individual soul. To be effective this would require a group of especially selected men of unusual caliber, equipment and vision to devote their lives to this planning.

Some of the things to be taken care of would be the working out for industry of effective methods for elimination of monopolistic practices of both management and labor, federal guaranteed jobs for all unemployed persons at wages low enough to encourage return to private employment, and incentive taxation to encourage progress and useful employment.

The perfect harmonizing of these four parts would consist of achieving the highest objectives of each one, by means of selecting and blending together the best parts of the various methods suggested. The chief problem in achieving this orchestration will be to harmonize the Radical and Conservative (the Bass and the Baritone). I shall therefore consider them together. How can we draw forth the *best* in two diametrically opposed viewpoints and *blend* them together? When this is done our song of harmony should be complete.

The radical wants work for all and security for all, while the conservative wants protection of private capital and the encouragement of private enterprise. Why should these two ends be mutually exclusive? Why cannot we promote an economic system that will furnish every man, woman and child reasonable economic security against unemployment, want and poverty, and at the same time furnish reasonable opportunity for the development of his talents and his capacities for creativity and advancement?

This could be achieved by dividing our economy into two distinct areas—first, a socialized area dealing with all the projects which the people should have but are not willing to pay for through the price system of private enterprise; and secondly, a private area of freedom and individual initiative for all production and for all projects which people want and are willing to pay for through the price system of private enterprise. The carefully planned government would provide temporary employment and purchasing power for all who might otherwise be unemployed, until such time as they could be placed in private enterprise. Hence unemployment would be completely eliminated but with private enterprise still functioning.

In a political democracy there is a perfect understanding between the areas of Freedom and the areas of Control. A person doesn't have freedom of choice whether he shall pay his taxes or not—it is absolutely required, that he shall pay them, and there is no "ifs" or "ands" about it. This requirement is completely under the jurisdiction and control of the State. When it comes to choice of religions he has absolute freedom of choice and the government has no control over him whatsoever. To mix a little freedom and a little control in each would be like mixing white and black paint until there is neither black nor white but merely a dirty gray. We want hot water for our tea and cold water for our lemonade; we don't want to compromise with tepid water for each.

In the past we have tried mixtures in our economic

system—now let us try organization and balance. For instance, where all industry was organized for profit and the unemployed were given free handouts, we had a mixture that was not conducive to free democracy, but degrading to real manhood.

A dole in money, which was not earned, to buy food from a "profit-making" grocer, who was going bankrupt, is not balanced democracy, but a mongrel state, neither true socialism nor true capitalism.

I shall not here try to indicate all of the projects which should be socialized—we should create a permanent planning board of the most able and practical men to do this. To make this plan, indicated above, work, there should be a separate department of government which could plan years in advance— a "department for looking ahead"—to work toward two objectives, namely, the completion of socially desirable projects which are not forthcoming through private enterprise governed by the incentives of the price system, and secondly, the furnishing, through these projects, of useful temporary employment for all unemployed persons. The building of highways, schools, hospitals, colleges, research laboratories, libraries, experimental farms, cultural facilities, parks, playgrounds, trade schools, museums of science and health, the tearing down of slums and building of modern apartment areas in their places, possibly even

the building of churches and cathedrals—these **are**
some activities that might be suggested.

The blending and harmonizing of the First and
Second Tenor (the individual and group idealist)
will be much easier. One is primarily interested in
saving the individual for his highest destiny, through
finding his perfect relationship to God, and the other
is primarily interested in saving and improving the
race to achieve the finest fruits of the brotherhood
of man. Both are interested in developing, by pre-
cept and above all by example, a better breed of spiritual men: men who put first things first, place the
spiritual and ethical always at the top and relegate
the lesser things, such as possessions, prestige, place
and position, to subordinate positions, where they
cannot rise up and pollute the pure springs of spirit.

Opportunities should be given adequately by
means of communal farms or hillside huts, places of
relief, for those who crave the more aesthetic life,
whether in loneliness or in communal and co-
operative societies, to find full expression for their
cravings.

Whether such stiff discipline, such high ideals of
sainthood as practiced by Saint Francis, Gandhi, and
Tolstoy, are practical and achievable for the general population is questionable, but there is no doubt

whatever that the leavening influence of those comparatively few individuals who can attain this ideal is one of the most **precious** and valuable possessions that any nation or community can boast. And it is equally undeniable that there are many rare and saintly souls who can and do attain this state of high and selfless leavening power who do not find it necessary to go through all the austere rigors of a Saint Francis. Such persons achieve this ideal of spiritual attainment while using means of the other orchestral group: possessing things without being possessed by them, doing business as a sacrament of the Lord, raising families to His glory, living godlike lives in purity and joyousness without giving to the devil anything that will contribute to the fullness of the happiness of man here and now. The fostering and developing of such a breed of men could well be made a major objective of any plan for solving the problems of the world.

While stimulus should be given to the development and adequate self-expression and loving service of these disciples of Saint Francis, these Friends, these Brothers of the Cross, adequate provision should be made by the State for the careful selection and perpetuation of a body of unusually gifted and consecrated and trained spiritual experts to work out a system of long-time planning for the development and improvement of the race.

This book does not pretend to present a final solution for the economic order. One thing I do know with absolute certainty, however, and that is that the solution must start in prayer. It must take its rise out of the orchestration of many people of many different views, melting and merging their views into the great Plan that God has in mind. And that Plan will finally emerge when enough of the people pray in sufficient harmony and faith and love. There is nothing that can stop it. We live in God's world and He can take care of His own when we take our little selves sufficiently out of the way.

XII. Praying for World Peace

War is not a disease, it is a symptom.

Fever in the body, even a high fever of 104 and 105 is never a disease, it is merely a symptom. The real disease is the cancer of hate, the goiter of envy, and the asthma of self-pity. These diseases cause the fever in the body. These same diseases cause war among the nations.

How can we cure fevers? By draining out the poisons of hate, envy and self-pity.

How can we end wars? By draining out the poisons of injustice, discord, fear and hate. And the place to begin putting the converse of these into expression—harmony, trust and love—is in ordering the economic affairs of all nations so that the causes of war may be forever eliminated. There is no other way. That is, if we wish the next peace to be a permanent peace and not merely an armistice or a truce.

Indeed, if we dream, work and pray until we bring an unselfish economic system into every nation and into the world, one root cause of all the world's injustice would be removed.

But in the meantime, before all the world's injustices have been corrected, all the discords ironed out, all the fears allayed and all the hate turned into love, how shall we defend ourselves? With armies? With navies? With airplanes? Until justice is done to all the weaker nations by the stronger nations I cannot conscientiously urge any nation to disarm. But I can recommend a more effective arming than any of the three branches of the fighting forces mentioned above.

In 1918 the armies controlled the trenches, the roads and the bridgeheads and the navy controlled the sea lanes. In 1942 it appears possible that those nations whose airplanes control the airways will win the war.

Let us step into the rhythm of this upward movement which has swept up from the land and sea into the sky, and see if there are any unknown powers above the skies which shall have a more decisive influence upon the outcome of wars in the future than any of the forces that we have hitherto known.

As we trust to battleships today, the ancients put their trust in horses; as we trust armored tanks today, the ancients put their trust in chariots. Listen now to the words of the prophet Isaiah: "Woe to them that go down to Egypt for help, and rely on horses, and trust in chariots because they are many, and in horsemen because they are very strong, but they look not unto the Holy One of Israel, neither seek Jehovah! As birds hovering, so will Jehovah of hosts protect Jerusalem; he will protect and deliver it, he will pass over and preserve it." (Isaiah 31:1,5) If we trust utterly to the Lord, His weapons will protect, deliver, and preserve us!

There is one advantage which the weapons of the Lord have over the weapons of men. The weapons of men are continually changing. In the far past they were sling shots, then bows and arrows, swords, spears, and battering rams. Then they became muskets, hand grenades, powder and shot. Now they are tanks, bombs, machine guns and hidden mines. Tomorrow they may be big black pills, which, when dropped from sufficient height, will blow up London and Berlin with one blast; or electric vibrators, which, when properly manipulated will shock an army of a million men into instant death. Every year the weapons of the past year become obsolete. An entire new technique must be mastered by the army overnight.

But the weapons of the Lord never become obsolete. Once learn them and a power is ours which will always protect, deliver and preserve us!

I do not believe in running away from danger. I do not believe in surrendering to savagery. I don't believe in appeasing evil. There are many things—

in ourselves as well as in others—which I believe in resisting with every pound of energy that we possess.

But I am just a little bit finicky about my choice of weapons, that is all.

I don't like bombs because they blow people to little bits and leave a lot of grease around. And they blow up property so that when the war is over inflation comes into the country, and finally spreads to my own country, and throws me out of work, too.

I don't like machine guns because they mow down fair-haired boys that look exactly like my own boy, turning them into fertilizer in the twinkling of an eye, or leaving them to rot in veteran hospitals for the rest of their lives. And I love boys, no matter where they come from, and I can't get over loving them.

But with all my prejudice against bombs and with all my love for boys I might still give up my aversion to the conventional weapons of war if I did not know of some other weapons for stopping evil infinitely more powerful than these weapons can ever pretend to be.

The weapons I believe in are Faith and Love. These, I believe, are the weapons of the Lord.

I have seen the power of these weapons when Jacob, returning to his native land rich with cattle and sheep, found himself confronted with Esau with four hundred armed men, and a vow in his heart to kill the man who had defrauded him of his birthright. I have seen Jacob take his wives and his children up into a mountain and there, surrounded with everyone who was near and dear to him, put on a love broadcast that turned back the sword of destruction.

An angel of the Lord wrestled with him throughout the night, and at dawn stretched out his hand upon him and lamed him for life, so that henceforth he could no longer fight even if he had wished. The next morning Jacob sent great gifts of sheep and cattle as outer expressions of his love and repentance to his brother. When he followed after, expecting to meet his death, instead he found his brother returning the gifts, and running to embrace him.

I have seen love look out from the eyes of Stephen as he said to his executioners, "Lord, lay not this sin to their charge." And I have seen Saul, the man who hounded Stephen to his death, the greatest Gestapo agent of his day, who threw Jews into concentration camps and who held their clothes while his followers stoned them to death—I have seen this Hitler of his day stricken down by a bolt of light and become the greatest disciple that the Christian church has ever known.

I have seen a Man on a cross in his suffering, after he had been betrayed and scourged and crucified for sins which He Himself did not commit, cry out, "Forgive them, Father, for they know not what they do." I have seen that Man conquer the world.

Unless one has been trained consciously to the point where he believes nay, *knows*—that Love is the most powerful force in the universe, it would be quite useless for me to counsel him to exchange bombs and machine guns for Love. We would all admit, I am sure, that it would be folly for every soldier to start off as a pilot of an airplane before he had been trained in the consciousness and technique of flying. I, who *know* from experience that Love and Prayer are more powerful than bombs and airplanes, also know that for a man who was not trained in consciousness to the point where he believes— nay, *knows*—that Love is the strongest force in the universe, and who is not trained in the art and technique of prayer it would be folly to expose his loved ones to the attacks of the enemy. It is not for me to say that a man should not take up arms and fight if his conscience says that he should do so. It is not for me to say that a nation is entirely sold out to Satan if it turns itself into an armed camp. It is only for me to bear witness with the utmost power which I possess, to that which I have actually seen with my own eyes and experienced in my own soul. And that witness bears positive and, for me, convincing evidence that the most powerful and irresistible weapons are the weapons of Prayer and Love.

One good feature about this way of fighting I am advocating is this: when you win, you win permanently, and you will never experience what the allies experienced after their "victory" of Versailles. And what is still more important, even when you lose, you still *win*, as witness Stephen overcoming Saul of Tarsus at the price of his own death, and Jesus overcoming the world at the price of the cross. Many today are armed to kill; let us help the nation and the world by arming ourselves to Love and Pray.

While I am confident that most of you who have patiently read into this book this far will follow me the rest of the way, yet it is possible that some others will exclaim at this point, "But this is too fantastic for words, even to suggest that the Lord could by some weird words of magic, some incantation, some presto-changeo, throw back a blitzkrieg supported by planes, tanks, and fast-moving trained soldiers! The Lord is always on the side of the heaviest battalions." To this we can only reply, "We are not talking of magic. God works by laws. And just as the laws of health are influenced by laws of right thinking and right acting, so all the other works of God are governed by laws of right thinking and right acting."

In the larger cosmic sense nations are not defeated by other nations; they defeat themselves. Neither does God bring calamities upon nations; they bring calamities upon themselves. Here are some of the instruments by which God allows nations to defeat themselves.

1. By earthquake. In 1923, at a time when there was very intense agitation and bitterness between Japan and the United States, and when there was much talk of the possibility of war between the two, there came that great earthquake, which reduced Japan in one night from a first-class fighting nation to a third-class nation. Moreover, the immediate and spontaneous response to this from the citizens of America in the way of generous gifts of money and supplies, or prayers and goodwill, did more than a dozen earthquakes could have done, to wipe away the bogy of war for almost twenty years.

Knowing how the delicate instruments of the radio vibrate to the voices of people thousands of miles away, may it not be possible to conceive that the fluid and heated mass at the center of the world might be more vibrant to the emotions and vibrations of the human mind than we at present may be aware of? At any rate, the human hearts, which vibrate to the needs of the victims of the earthquake become mighty forces toward peace on earth.

Japan is built over one of the very worst earthquake "faults," as they are called, on the earth. A very slight shake would tumble down the flimsy buildings, the factories, the shipyards, and remove Japan's striking power instantly. If the Lord wanted to stop the war He could very easily do it, as easily as a man, sleeping, could shake the sand off his face by a mild shaking of his being.

2. By pestilence. Pestilence always follows wars, and very often accompanies them, especially when they are long drawn out. This is brought about chiefly by the weakening resistance caused by lack of proper food, exhaustion and the prolonged exposure of the body to privations, and of the mind to the chaotic emotions of fear, hate, and despair. When the Assyrians came down like a wolf on the fold in the time of Isaiah, they were rolled back from Jerusalem by the epidemic which struck them. When the German hosts were drawing close to Paris in the second battle of the Marne, the dread influenza epidemic weakened them so severely that they could not carry on.

We hear much of the *ten* million boys who lost their lives fighting in the first World War; little mention is made of the *twenty* million people who lost their lives in the influenza epidemic which followed the war. Where the battlefield slays its thousands, the pestilence slays its tens of thousands.

3. By snow and rain, drouth and floods. Napoleon's power was not crushed at Waterloo; it was destroyed in the Russian snows. Of the 500,000 picked men who marched on Moscow, 20,000 returned. The snows and cold of Russia have done more to break the power of Hitler than all the armies of the allies combined. As the Lord holds the threat of an earthquake, like a Damocles sword, over the head of Japan, He holds the threat of Russian snows above the head of the German armies.

4. By turning upon one's own partners. The ten thousand Midianites were thus destroyed in the presence of the three hundred men of Gideon. When Germany turned upon Russia in the summer of 1941 we had a similar situation.

5. By destroying one's own key leaders and raising up great leaders for the enemy. The death of Stonewall Jackson, "Lee's right hand," by one of his own pickets sealed the fate of the South. The rise of a great military genius like Foch in the first World War sealed the fate of Germany. The removal, by Hitler, of the remarkable military genius Field Marshal Walther von Brauchitsch who brought

about the defeat of Poland and shortly thereafter, of all of France; and the rise of Bleucher, the Siberian general of Russians, to lead the winter armies around Moscow to a great victory, are examples in modern times.

6. By the conversion of the leaders to be friends of the enemy. Esau was won over to be a friend of Jacob. Saul of Tarsus, the worst Gestapo agent and ruthless destroyer of the Christians ever known, was suddenly changed to be their greatest champion of the Christian church. If a leader should rise and take control of the German nation and then become completely converted to the ideals of democracy and turn and become our friend, this would be the finest miracle of all the miracles that we could possibly ask the Lord to bring to pass. Such a way to end war would have seeds of permanence.

To change the hearts of men would be an infinitely greater miracle of God than to bring the earthquakes, snows, pestilence, and enemy discords to save us.

Suffice to say, there are sufficient channels for the Lord to act through, and act decisively, as He has very often done, in the past. In fact, few are the wars in history, where Chance, Fate, or Providence (whatever you wish to call it) has not had a major share.

But far, far more important for us to understand

than merely the instruments that the Lord could use to end a war, are the methods by which man by prayer can help bring about changes in his own heart and in the hearts of his own countrymen, by which the need of war to settle disputes will end forever.

Wars are brought upon nations because of their sins. We have all departed from God. We nations that have been blessed above all others in material wealth, insofar as we have exploited weaker nations and let greed control our actions, also have need of repentance as much as any of the rest if we would be immune to the laws of the pestilence and the laws of the sword.

The initial sin of Germany is not that she adopted Nazism. Anyone knowing the bankrupt and well-nigh hopeless condition of Germany in 1933, her needs ignored by the democracies, will well know that she had only two choices, Nazism or Communism. Many think—considering the limitation of choice—that she chose the right thing. Her sin was that she tried to retaliate with hate, and by making all other nations mere means to serve her selfish ends, she threw aside the laws of God for the laws of man.

Had Hitler kept the promise he made at Munich to take no more land by conquest after receiving the slice of Sudetenland, he would have been the greatest figure in Europe, and Germany would have been the dominant power for the next hundred years. Never in history was there so signal a diplomatic victory won so easily as that which he won over Chamberlain and Daladier. Every little nation would have climbed on his band wagon. No one would have dared dispute him. Had he gone on to make Europe one great economic union, even though he made Germany for a time the chief beneficiary, all Europe would have acquiesced. Ultimately—for in time fairness and justice will prevail—all nations would have come into an equal and satisfactory place in the European alliance.

If this war today that we are preparing to sacrifice the lives of our innocent boys for, and perhaps even wreck our present type of economic system to win, turns out to be a war staged by our own money powers to save their particular type of economic security, if we find later on that our own selfishly high tariffs have been strangling the life out of weaker nations, in short, if we, like Germany, plan to use other nations as mere means to serve our selfish ends, then we shall have to pay as awful a price as Germany will pay. The only way to escape paying that price is not so much by building more warships, planes and tanks and guns, as by turning in penitence to our Father and asking Him to cleanse our ways. The most patriotic prayer that we can pray in this day and hour is not for a million boys in the opposing armies to be destroyed by our guns, but for our own evils to be cleaned out and a new America to be born. The very day that all evil shall be cleaned out of this nation the war will end. The Lord will use His earthquake, His snows, His pestilence, His discord in the ranks of the enemy, or He will lift up leaders in our midst who will lead us to victory, or He will so change the hearts of our enemies that they will come into fraternal accord in bringing about a peace, merciful and just to all.

Epilogue

Are we asking too much? Does it seem fantastic and unreasonable to consider seriously using the power of the infinite heavens for the problems of this little earth? To this all I can reply is, Have our other reliances been so successful that we need spurn this?

Again I am asked, Is not this bordering upon superstition to lean so utterly upon the promises of a Sacred Book? To this I can reply, Should we not at least give as fair a trial to the revelations of Jesus as we do to the discoveries of Edison and Marconi.

Again someone may ask, What is the use of starting another movement? People have started such things from the beginning of time and what good came of them? A little shouting and blowing of trumpets, a few sporadic organizations, and the thing will die, just as all other movements have died before it.

To this let me reply as I have stated before, This is not a Movement that anyone is starting, least of all the author of this little book. It is a Movement which has been going on for centuries, but which few of us have properly recognized, and fewer still have tried to put ourselves in alignment with. It is a movement as permanent and as continuous as the flow of the Mississippi River toward the sea. For thousands, yes, millions of years, the Father of Waters has been flowing in its course. But only comparatively very recently have men learned how to utilize it to light their homes and run their factories. All through the ages it has been there, flowing past our doors, but we have not recognized it, except as something to amuse us when we wished to go fishing or swimming, or as something to disturb and obstruct us when we wanted to go over to the other bank, or as something to entertain or thrill us with its beauty and picturesqueness when we rested our eyes upon its landscape.

In a similar manner we have turned to the stories in the Scriptures as something to amuse us at the bedtime hour, as something to disturb and obstruct us when we wanted to achieve some selfish end contrary to its rigid code, or as something to stir us by its beauty when we wanted to garnish a poem or inspire an audience. But as something to light our homes or turn the machinery of our business and of our nation, it would be folly even to think of such a thing!

It seems that it is only when a man and his race

are in danger of ultimate destruction that he turns to the Father in Heaven for purposes other than to amuse, obstruct, or thrill. Have we not now reached a time in history when we need all the Light and Power that a Heavenly Father can give? Let us consider this Power and all that it can mean to us.

The omnipotent Power of God, let me repeat, is as simple and as natural and yet as continuous and as permanent as the flow of a river toward the ocean.

I have stood beside the Mississippi, I have followed the track of the Missouri and the Ohio, I have traveled along the Rhine and the Thames and the Elbe and the Po. Some of these rivers flow east, some west, some north and some south. But they all sooner or later find the path which destiny has granted to them and they all some day find their way to the sea.

What is it that drives them toward their goal? The slope of the ground, the tip of the earth? They flow downward, you say? But what do you mean by downward? Pick up this globe and turn it around and around, looking at the rivers as marked upon it. When tipped in one direction the Missouri River should flow east, when tipped in another it should flow west. "But," you interrupt me, "by flowing downward I didn't mean down in space but down toward the center of the earth." Ah, that is different, for that is not down at all, at least down only half of the twenty-four hours. What you mean is not *down* but *toward the center*. The rivers flow in the direction of the center of the earth.

What drives them there? Nothing drives them there. *Something draws them there*. What can that drawing be? We, with our little limited mental outlook, our impoverished condition of understanding, call it by a big word which none of us—not even the wisest of us—understands, *Gravity*. What is gravity? It is the great drawing power which draws all things on earth into harmony and guides everything on earth to its goal—that is all that we know.

Let us leave now this little subject of rivers, interesting as it is, and let us turn our thoughts to a far greater theme—the eternal flow of human consciousness within us all—the rivers of the Soul. What is it that draws us into the place where the rhythm of the ages means for us to be drawn, what is it that draws us out of all our troubles, all our illnesses, all our sufferings, into perfect harmony, perfect happiness, perfect self-expression? Here again it is not a driving, but a drawing, and here again I must use a word which we, in our limited understanding, do not understand at all, even the wisest among us do not understand—*Love*. All we know is that love is the power that draws all men into perfectly adjusted and harmonious relationship with everyone else. It is the place of perfect peace, perfect happiness, and perfect concord.

Now let us put down the globe which we have been holding while demonstrating this great law which regulates the flow of the rivers, and let us pick up the magnet, the smallest and most typical symbol of that great unexplainable force which men call gravity. The drawing power of gravity at the center of the earth and the drawing power of the little magnet we hold in our hand is one and the same thing. The magnet is a bent piece of steel united at one end, but in the form of two separate pieces at the other end. Two pieces of steel united as one! Both are magnetized, but both would lose their magnetism if deprived for any length of time from the presence or proximity of the other.

Now let us turn from the great impersonal force of *Love* which we mentioned a moment ago in the same breath with the law of Gravity, resting at the center of the universe, and seek love as objectified and incarnate in human beings. For as gravity, when sufficiently slowed down finds its expression in the humble magnet, so God's Love ultimately finds its expression in the humble love of man for man. For as the magnet is two prongs of steel united above as one, so Love on earth finds its perfect expression in two human personalities who are aware that they are united as one in harmony in God above.

Thus we see where two or three gather together that there is a magnet which draws down the answer from heaven. Just as one prong of the magnet is magnetized and can draw unto itself for awhile but ultimately loses this power unless in close juxtaposition to the opposite prong, so one person who separates himself from his fellows can draw answers to prayer for awhile, but if he continues to shut his love life off from his fellow men he will soon find that the power is fading out of his prayer. And why? Simply because he ceases to be magnetized with Love. A man who was born and lived all his life on a desert island without ever meeting or knowing a human being would become brutalized simply because he would never really know what *love* was. The virtue of two coming together, especially if they are in such deep inner harmony that they can "agree as to what they shall ask for," lies in the power that comes from the polarization of their love. When one unlocks the door to another's love he is simply unlocking the power of Gravity which draws all things unto itself. For God is Love and Love is merely the heavenly aspect of Gravity. Therefore when Jesus said, "If but two of you on earth agree as to what you shall pray for, whatever it be, it will be granted you by the Father who is in Heaven," He might have said, "It will be *drawn* to you by the Father."

When two or three or more come together in a Prayer Group in the spirit of love and harmony, recognizing the fact that they are united above as one, then it is that they are releasing the power of Spiritual Gravity that draws all things into perfectly adjusted and harmonious relationship with everything else.

Such a group can truly *agree* on what they should ask for. And by agree I don't mean mere intellectual agreement, but I mean rather that deeper agreement of the heart that brings them into perfect harmony and accord upon the matter they seek. Such agreement is not for selfish reasons but in order to bring greater harmony into the world in accordance with the larger Plan of God, whatever that Plan may be. Such an agreement means that they have come together in that sense of perfect unity with each other and with God that constitutes the coming together in "Christ's Name" or in His Nature, "hid with Christ in God." A group coming together in this spirit can rightfully avail itself of the power contained in Jesus' promise, "Whatsoever ye ask agreeing in My Name will be done."

When Christ said, "Abide in Me as I abide in the

Father and He in Me," He was stating the law of spiritual magnetism and spiritual gravity, which, when properly experienced, and properly released in this world through man's love for his fellow man, will draw all our activities into perfect harmony, perfect peace, and perfect love.

Let us in this spirit, in our Quiet Hour and in our Prayer Groups, take all those that we love and all those who reach out to us for help, and one by one, give them to the drawing power of the Love of God. Let us, finally, take our nation and our world deeply into our hearts, and give them also into the flow of God's infinite Love.

If it will help to focus our thought and give us the consciousness that we are uniting in prayer with hundreds of others, let us for several days, or, if we wish, for several weeks, unite in offering the following prayer:

Our Heavenly Father,

Knowing that Thou art the God of Love, Giver of every good and perfect gift, and that Thy Love is the greatest of all drawing powers, infinite, eternal, and irresistible, drawing all things into perfect harmony and perfect fulfillment, we give ourselves completely into Thy Hands. Take us, mold us, shape us into channels for expressing Thy will.

[153]

Knowing that where two or three come together and agree, asking anything in the consciousness of Oneness with Jesus Christ, that their prayer will be answered, we especially pray for the spirit of Christ's Love to take such complete control of our hearts that we may be able to pray for a peace that will be a blessing both to our friends and to our enemies; for a prosperity that will begin in the soul and extend to the needs of the mind and the body as well; and finally that there will be raised up men of vision in places of power who will bring the spirit of Christ into all walks of life, so that the Prince of Peace may be ruler in all the councils of nations, and in the hearts of men everywhere.

In Christ's Name, Amen.